T0147468

Stand while I
sentence you...

Stand while I
sentence you...

Tony Morich

Order this book online at www.trafford.com
or email orders@trafford.com

Most Trafford titles are also available at major online book retailers.

Disclaimer: A True Story… listed as a work of fiction, due to legal reasons.

Printed in the United States of America.

ISBN: 978-1-4669-1237-3 (sc)
ISBN: 978-1-4669-1238-0 (e)

Trafford rev. 01/30/2012

 www.trafford.com

North America & International
toll-free: 1 888 232 4444 (USA & Canada)
phone: 250 383 6864 ♦ fax: 812 355 4082

CONTENTS

FOREWORD

The Lord to me; "Isn't that what you are, Tony? A writer? SO WRITE!"

God made heaven and God made hell and God made THIS world—the earth realm reality that we live in due to our spirit being encased in our physical flesh body—which is a temporary situation for all of us. Due to all of what you will read about in this book—I praise the Lord for only passing through this world.

What we do in THIS world determines where we go and to which world we will go to next. A lot of it is up to you. So don't act like a damn nut! God wishes for no one to perish, but for you to repent and turn from your sins.

I was suicidal, homicidal—all from facing false charges brought against me which totaled 50 years in prison. God HIMSELF intervened and used a great trajedy—my 8 years of wrongful imprisonment—to produce an important storybook—the book you are reading now.

You can't just go BANG and kill someone or yourself and then die and wonder what is next and you are sorry and then it is too late. The judgment rushes upon you—not from corrupt man—but from a Pure, True, Righteous ALL POWERFUL, ALL KNOWING GOD. There is no where to run or hide and money does not exist to save you. The blood shed on the cross by JESUS CHRIST should come to your mind right now. Whatever God does with your soul is right because He made it. God is perfect and needs not to change. We are imperfect and NEED to change. The red lettered words in the bible are what we need to heed—the words of JESUS CHRIST—our role model. More of you Lord and less of me. Judgment is by Christ and is done as only He can. Vengence with Love is a perfect Just balance. I prefer more of the love side myself—but that is up to you also by how your performance in this world is carried out. The eyes of the Lord are everywhere watching the wicked and the good. It is a fearful thing to fall into the hands of the living God as we all will someday.

The world and all of us need to learn these things. Pay attention! There is a test on all of this—it is called the rest of your life. These words are not my own and I do not take credit for them. I'm just the tool in these pages.

Let our book begin . . . A TRUE STORY . . . that the world needs to hear.

INTRODUCTION

June 12, 2011. God always existed with no beginning and no end. We are created beings with a physical start and finish, so at times it is difficult for us to understand God. Being that our flesh bodies pass by and are either burned up—cremation—or are buried; because of this—we need to pay attention to our SOUL DIRECTION. Where is our soul/spirit going to, after we die? The Judgment.

"Moreover, the Father judges no one, but has entrusted all judgment to the Son." John 5:22.

So I would say it would be good to follow Jesus Christ and to represent Him, as opposed to His enemy—The devil. They are both very real, as I personally know. If you claim to have met Jesus or the devil, the public eye would say that you are crazy. Even though, people still claim to hear the voice of

God. Either a small quiet voice, or a powerful and loud one, as many of you reading now can attest to.

This book is to wake you up! I usually say it different when speaking to people in person. This book is not about me—at all. It is about what God can do and how real He is. God can do ANYTHING. He is all powerful, everywhere at the same time, see's all, knows all, hears all. I don't know of any superhero who can do all of that.

We are called to be perfect, as He is perfect. He cannot lie, so we also should speak the truth. God can help you no matter where you are, because He is there with you. The jail part of the book is included as a CRIME PREVENTION measure. Believe me, you don't want to do 8 years in the State Pennitentiary like I did. I'll tell you all about it so you can skip it in your life. Hopefully you will turn away from crime or stop hanging around the wrong people—which is what I was guilty of.

In this book, my first of many, Jesus is the star, Sammy is my brother—that I didn't know I had, and I'm just the tool to make it all readable, knowing that we who teach will be judged more strictly.

CHAPTER 1

The corrupt legal process

I wrote chapters 1 through 5 while still in the jail, because when you get out—your mind makes you forget all the trauma, drama, the babys' mama, and all the craziness that happened day by day. It definitely shortens your lifespan from the noise. Doors banging, people yelling, the shakedowns, lockdowns, the fact that a third of the population-of 2000 prisoners—have either hepatitis, aids, or other physical or mental problems that can rub off on you. Not everyone makes it out alive and no one wants to die in the jail.

"My minimum is double digits!", my one friend would tell me. "I'm gonna die in this place!" I would hear a lot of that.

The Lord knows what you're going through.

I was thrown away from 1999 to 2007. But God says to bloom where you are planted. Everyone had to see the psych. He would tell us that you are still in the world, but your world simply got smaller. It's like being at the high school with a big double razor wire fence all around it, and you simply have to stay there.

I call this chapter as it is. How about the illegal legal system? I read in the newspaper that a federal judge quit because he refused to be a part of an unjust justice system. I didn't say it—he said it. Well praise the Lord. We all know that man and woman do the best that they can and also that absolute power corrupts absolutely. Remember the British with the taxes you had to pay. They were allowed to stay in your house, have sex with your wife, take your money, take your freedom, take your life. So the mighty America said "NO MORE." Praise the Lord for George Washington being a Christian and God making us a great nation. But now we are the British.

After rereading what I wrote while in the jail, I see that I bashed a lot of people, and every word of it was true. God knows the evil they did to me, so my comfort is to not exploit them, but to give it all to the Lord knowing that these people will stand before the Lord after they physically die. Speaking of all the corrupt details will take our focus off of God, so we aint gonna go there! Thank you Jesus. We'll sum it up and say that I did 8 years for a crime I did not commit. Lord knows the truth, so why do you care what man thinks?

"And I saw something else under the sun; In the place of judgment-wickedness was there, in the place of justice-wickedness was there, I thought in my heart, God will bring to judgment both the righteous and the wicked, for there will be a time for every activity, a time for every deed." Ecclesiastes 3:16-17.

The trial was 5 days and I was found not guilty of 4 big charges, then the jury compromised the verdict and stuck me with one felony and 8 years. The one felony was just the same as the 4 charges that they said not guilty of. But who cares and so what you have the right to appeal. We'll talk about that later. Now let's get to the good stuff—chapter 2.

CHAPTER 2

Welcome to jail!

"Now I want you to know, brothers, that what has happened to me has really served to advance the gospel." Phillipians 1:12

"Blessed is the man who perseveres under trial, because when he has stood the test, he will receive the crown of life that God has promised to those who love him." James 1:12

This is why it has been years later—that this book is finally being typed now. Who would want to relive all this crap? I thought the money was the obstacle. Nope, it was me.

After the guilty verdict, they took me away! I guess that says it all. To the county jail, Lord help us. Handcuffs and cop cars and tears and fears baby! I saw my family walking down the sidewalk with my one lawyer so I said to the driver, "Hey there's my family—beep the horn!" So the driver beeped and I'm trying to wave with the handcuffs on.

We got to the jail and they took my street clothes. Now I was property of the DOC. The beloved Department of Corrections. Guess they thought that I did something wrong so they now get their opportunity to correct a person. So we're gonna see what all of this is about, real shortly here. Strip search. I don't even care if that's a sentence fragment, it deserves to be by itself. Take all of your clothes off—butt naked. Put your arms out in front of you like you are some kind of zombie or something. Then! Turn your hands over, put your hands up over your head, and we aint finished yet. Open your mouth and lift your tongue up. "Anything underneath there Morich?" It gets better. Then they look behind your ears. Turn around and lift up your feet. Then they tell you to bend over and spread your butt cheeks so they can see if there are any weapons up there. Then you're done. If you are a female prisoner, they have to look in female places. Now that wasn't so bad, was it? You've only been in jail for 5 minutes, and what do you mean—you don't like it?

So I'm at the jail having an anxiety attack like the other 98% of the new arrivals. We can go on and on about this stuff, but I'm trying to have a 100 page book.

Everyone is scared at first, but you learn to adapt to the new environment. Hope you like iron and concrete. Man made hell—the jail—bloom where you are planted.

I was at the county jail for 60 days. No sunlight. You don't go outside. Your skin turns white. No real fresh air because the windows don't open. Man oppressing men and women. Sure jails are needed, and I need to tell you all of this because this is partly a CRIME PREVENTION book. TO WAKE YOU UP—you young future criminal that might be reading this book. Society deserves to be safe from the ones who are and do evil.

Sentencing day arrived and I thought, "He gonna cut me loose!" Not a snowballs chance in hell. But surely he had to know I was not guilty of the only one felony. There was no physical evidence to convict me—and no dna. I had plans for the night, for goodness sakes.

Drum roll please for the book title, "Stand while I sentence you.", the judge says." What's he talking about?", I asked my one lawyer. "You're being incarcerated.", he said. Well what the hell is that? I was about coronary. I think they want to see somebody fall over dead when they say that. But praise the

LORD! You will benefit from my pain, shame, blame, a victim of the game—is how other prisoners would describe it.

So, we're back to the county jail. Just another strip search—you should be getting used to it by now.

The pale colored people from no sun. The judge gave me a court appointed lawyer as the money ran out for the good lawyer. Then I knew I was really up the creek without a paddle, and without a boat. Later, I'll let you know just how messed up things became. No money, no honey, and it's not funny.

Soon after, I was moved to Western Pennitentiary in the beautiful city of Pittsburgh, Pa. Home of the champions and all you got to see was a wall and pigeon crap everywhere. I remember some football player somewhere accused of a rape charge—alledgedly—but you can't put a champion away and put him on no Megan Law. It just simply would not be the right thing to do. The fact that he had millions of dollars simply has nothing to do with any of it. As long as you say allegedly, it is all ok. Topics like this take our focus off of God.

You the prisoner and they are the CO—Correction Officer. I use improper English because this is how you start to talk, like the rest of the prisoners. In the old days, they would nail you to a cross, or impale you, or cut off your head, or line you up for a firing squad, or electrocute you. Man killing man. Now, they do something worse. Put you in a jail and throw away the key, and the minority of cases get overturned. But there is always hope to get out. God can do anything! I ended up in the hole. 23 hours a day locked in your room. Ice cold air blowing out of the air vent. No toilet paper. I had to wipe my butt with a sock, then rinse it out in the sink. Thank God for the sock! Just part of the torture.

In that room was a red bible. I still have it. I read like 140 pages in one day. The bible people were in the jail also, they probably didn't have toilet paper either. But God started working on me, on my spirit man. I learned to forgive those evil people down Western. God taught me that it is for Him to take revenge. He can do it and not get in any trouble for it.

"But I tell you who hear me: Love your enemies, do good to those who hate you, bless those who curse you, pray for those who mistreat you." Luke 6:27.

After my 10 days at Western, I was transported in the middle of the night with others to Camp Hill. They brought me a brown bag with 2 hard eggs, and a little thing of milk to prepare me for the journey. We arrived at Camp Hill, baby! One of the black prisoners said, "I think we gonna be ok, I see a brother in uniform!" Thank you Jesus. To tell you the truth, about 75 percent of the population in jail was/ is black. The black people were nicer to me than the white people. We'll get to all of that later.

At Camp Hill, I had a 74 year old celly. A celly is someone you live in the cell with. You learn to get along with total strangers and I definitely learned the importance of lifting weights at the yard. Do you hear what I'm saying Big Dog? Slim Jim aint gonna do it in the jail. Yes, my celly couldn't go to the bathroom for like 3 or 4 days at a time. I would call the nurse for him, fill papers out for him, do what Jesus would do—help somebody. The smell that would eminate from him was eye watering. He had the bottom bunk and I had the top one, and it was always an issue over the heat and air flow. That is just part of the torture. He was too hot and I was frozen with that wool blanket that I still have pieces of wool in my eyes from it. He wouldn't go to yard. He said there are killers out there! I reassured him that our walking group would keep him safe. That was an episode in itself.

You had four minutes for a shower at Camp Hill. It was called soap on and soap off. It was all very unhealthy. At the chow hall, when the guard walked over and knocked twice on your table—you were done eating whether you were done or not. The biggest waste of food I have ever seen, and people are starving in the world. Who cares so what—the taxpayers foot the bill. I was there for 3 months.

After that mess, they said, "Morich—you are going to ROCKVIEW!" The name even sounded scary. My celly had tears in his eyes when he watched me walk out. He was worried who the next celly would be. We boarded "The Blue Goose". The big blue bus full of prisoners, with an armed guard at the back in a cage area and the same for the front. Like someone was gonna fly in with an army helicopter and start rescuing us. Whatever! I heard the showers would be more than 4 minutes there and that's all that mattered. No wonder they had riots there many years ago. Flames and yelling and pain and hurt all because of how they ran it and talked to people, and treated you. You learn real quickly what the word RESPECT means. All the prisoners, mostly would talk right to each other. Respect, because you aint no better than me, and I aint no better than you. If you got a problem with your mouth, that can be fixed, as I saw a lot of fixing going on.

We arrived at Rockview, and that is where I met the Big Dog in the yard. Boy! Don't you cry Sammy when you read this! God knows I'm crying now. I'm walking around the yard all alone like a dog that was dropped off in the middle of nowhere. I see this big black guy walking over to me. So I'm thinking, "I can't beat this guy, so I better just talk nice to him." He says, "You look green!" I asked, "What is green?" He says, "Like a green leaf on a tree. New. New clothes, new number, NEW!" I said, "Where am I?' Sam introduced himself and explained that we are in the middle of Pa. I told him I don't know nothin' about this stuff. He says, "Boy! You at the college of knowledge. You didn't ask for this, but you got it. You can't buy this, you gotta earn it. The people who sent you here, don't care if you live or die, but I do."

Sam taught me there are 3 rules to survive. 1. Keep your mouth shut. 2. You do you. 3. Mind your own business. "You see all these people looking at us walking around here? Not one of them will bother you because they see you walking with me.", Sam told me. Thank you Jesus for Sam to teach me the things I never knew about jail. We'll get into more of this in a later chapter. Sam helped me carry my cross when it was too heavy for me to bear. A man named Simon, helped Jesus to carry His cross. Matthew 27:32.

CHAPTER 3

Focusing on God

This chapter is for you—you juvenile deliquent young criminal type and you—the crooked cop who pockets the money on the side. I don't blame you at all because every day that you put that badge on, you could be killed in the line of duty. Two of my friends are police officers. Yes sir! You see—I respect the law. The law kicked my ass, so you have to respect it and obey the laws, I did 8 years with no misconducts. I was in the hole at the start. I always figured that you were oppressed enough, so why let yourself be put in a cell for 23 hours a day? Oh, I did a lot of pushups. They made me so mad, I was gonna be Hercules when I got out.

This chapter is about your SOUL DIRECTION. Where is your soul going to after you die? Heaven is real and so is hell. Back me up, Lord!

"In hell, where he was in torment, he looked up and saw Abraham far away, with Lazarus by his side. So he called to him, "Father Abraham, have pity on me and send Lazarus to dip the tip of his finger in water and cool my tongue, because I am in agony in this fire." Luke 16:23-24.

Jesus said it. He can only tell the truth. All of our lives can be in a mess from time to time. For example: In my life, I was baptized at around ten years old as a Bible Baptist. All the church people sang by the side of the river; "Here we are gathered by the river . . ." My family took me to church and I remember attending Sunday school with the other kids when I was little. My family paid tithes and I had the perfect childhood. The Lord prevented the devourer from our lives.

"Return to me, and I will return to you," says the Lord Almighty. "But you ask, 'How are we to return?' "Will a man rob God? Yet you rob me, "But you ask, 'How do we rob you?' "In tithes and offerings. You are under a curse—the whole nation of you—because you are robbing me. Bring the whole tithe into the storehouse, that there may be food in my house. Test me in this," says the Lord Almighty, "and see if I will not throw open the floodgates of heaven and pour out so much blessing that you will not have room enough for it. I will prevent pests from devouring your crops, and the vines in your fields will not cast their fruit," says the Lord Almighty. "Then all the nations will call you blessed, for yours will be a delightful land," says the Lord Almighty. Malachi 3:7-12.

By the time I went to jail, I had to ask my mom, "Mom, these people want to know what religion I am, what do I put?" She says, "Well you are a Christian, Tony!" I'm sure glad she remembered. It's never been pretty when you tell people about your past life. Standing in front of the other 200 prisoners at the church, I told them how it was in 1990. I had a girlfriend who was a self-professed witch. We even had a felt painting on the living room wall of Satan. Little did I know at the time, that he only wants to kill, steal and destroy. The devil is the enemy. Him and his demons—all of which are real. Jesus speaks of these things.

Then Jesus was led by the Spirit into the desert to be tempted by the devil. Matthew 4:1

While they were going out, a man who was demon-possessed and could not talk was brought to Jesus. And when the demon was driven out, the man who had been mute spoke. The crowd was amazed and said, "Nothing like this has ever been seen in Israel." Matthew 9:32-33.

CHAPTER 4

The Things People Do In Jail

Sleep? Cry? Get beat up? Oh you'll find out after you read this chapter. The Lord is mighty to save. God gives you help along the way. Sammy Belle and others helped me in many ways.

The eyes of the Lord are everywhere, keeping watch on the wicked and the good. Proverbs 15:3.

Terminology—"Old head, young buck, babys' mom"; these are words I only heard of in jail. "Good lookin'!", means thank you. If someone gives you something, you say—good lookin'. "What he said—ya' heard?", "Knee-ya-mean?"-do you know what I mean? You see you end up talking like the people around you.

Spoon in the ice—This was always a big issue at the chow hall. Some people find it disrespectful if you sit down at the four people table and put your clean unused spoon in the water pitcher to get ice for your cup without first asking if anyone needs water. Even if you wipe off your clean unused spoon first! What about the block that just ate before you? Maybe they were yelling over the water pitcher with their mouths full of food, as they often do? I would rip my napkin in half and cover my cup for when people yell over your tray with their mouths full of food. They saw brother so and so in the chow line, so they have to yell to them. If you politely say something to them about it, a common response—after they glance at you to see how much muscles you have—would be, "Well, you in the jail!" Like that's a reason to be rude and have no manners? They think so.

Corn bread on the side of the head—Oh my goodies! This is a stupid one. Stupid is and stupid does—stupid things. We all need to pray daily for God to give us wisdom and knowledge. We try to do things our way and it just doesn't work out right. The Lords' ways are higher than mans' ways. One day I heard the guy at the table next to us, yelling-with his mouth full of food, of course—to his homey across the chow hall and I felt some chewed up corn bread hitting me on the left side of the head. He just looked at me as I gave him a disgusted look while wiping the side of my head off, and he got up and left. Lord let me bite my tongue. The goal was to go home. Some people were not taught manners. Some didn't have a mom or dad to teach them manners.

Three rules to survive—As Sammy said; 1. Keep your mouth shut. 2.Mind your own business. 3. You do you. Some people don't like it if you neb nose in their business. Some people never heard of a neb nose. That is someone who minds your business when they need to mind their own matters. It's a good way to get beat up or sadly killed if you are a police officer looking into someones personal business. It happens when the wrong person is being over-policed, and they go nuts. That's why you need to stay in the word and build your faith foundation on the rock—which is Jesus Christ. If you aint doing nothing wrong, then you aint got nothing to worry about. That's not always true.

Crapolla watchers—Tell it like it is, Tony! A staff person pushed my blanket off my door bars when I was going to the bathroom #2. They can look over and see if you are alive or not but if you touch my blanket, we got a problem. So I went after the new unit manager, who later we all found out he was gay and trying to get a free look at somebody. He got fired 'cause everyone went to the shift commander and the white hats about him. A white hat is a Lieutenant. Some staff people don't like the other ones.

The ladder Olympics—Sometimes the person on the top bunk seems like they are training for the ladder Olympics. Up and down, all day long. Practicing for the four counts they do every day? The count times are roughly 6am, 1pm, 6pm, and 9pm every day, day after day, year after year. When's it end? When you walk out that front gate.

30 years to go and can't wait 5 minutes—Some people there have big time and man are they IMPATIENT! When we would lift weights, they couldn't wait 5 seconds until you moved from the weight bench. People always jump line at the chow hall due to impatience.

20 wild horses peeing in a field—It is like waking up in an out house everyday. You live in a bathroom with a toilet and a sink. When certain cellys wake up and perform their marathon urinations, it is similar to the title of this paragraph. A courtesy flush half way through is sometimes needed. It's also a good idea to check the toilet after you use it. Why should your celly have to clean up your bodily mess?

Pooping limits per day—BIG ISSUE! "You already went once today!" Some people act like it is a major crisis if they have to step out of the cell for a few minutes. If the door is locked—like for count time—people should understand if you have irregular bowel movements. They figure—you can do what I do, just do it less.

Cell hogs—Everyone needs time alone and no one wants to look at their celly 24 hours a day. Give the other person some space. Go to block out, yard out, library, anywhere!

Something Wong—Yes W-O-N-G. I'm not rippin' on nobody here. My one Asian celly would tell me that I should go to sick call because I go to the bathroom twice a day. But it's ok when he has to pee every half hour and get up three times a night to pee, flush, and wash his hands.

The used tooth brush—Hold on to your imaginations. No one likes a tight wad or stingy person. Some people are so tight, their wallets squeak. One celly—gee, I can't think of his name—well I threw away my toothbrush one day into our cell garbage bag and he went right into the garbage and picked it up, held it up to me and said, "There's nothing wrong with this toothbrush, I'll just rinse it off and use it!" I tried to reason with him but he insisted it would save him .78 cents. He had about 200 dollars on his account. Being cheap can be very unattractive and very unhealthy.

Sink spitters—for and against—When I went to jail, people didn't spit in the sink, because that is where most people wash out their white boxer shorts after the shower. Now the new breed that went through when I was leaving, love to spit in the sink. They would reason with you and say, "Well you wash your underwear in their!" This will always be a topic of debate.

In the way—If your celly goes to yard for two hours, you know when they will return so don' be at the sink, taking a pee, or in your damn cabinet! Be out of the way, you had two hours to do you!

Hygienically challenged—Some people need politely told about the daily necessity of brushing their teeth—and brush your tongue for goodness sakes! That's where the stink comes from! Wear deodorant, take a shower, change your clothes, turn in dirty laundry, change your bed sheets. Be polite, but informative.

Turn from ALL of your sins—God doesn't want anyone to perish but to repent and turn from your sins. To sin is to break the law of God. These laws are necessary to repeat until you have them memorized:

Deuteronomy 5:6-22. "I am the Lord your God, who brought you out of Egypt, out of the land of slavery.

"You shall have no other gods before me.

"You shall not make for yourself an idol in the form of anything in heaven above or on the earth beneath or in the waters below. You shall not bow down to them or worship them; for I, the Lord your God, am a jealous God, punishing the children for the sin of the fathers to the third and fourth generation to those who hate me, but showing love to a thousand generations of those who love me and keep my commandments.

"You shall not misuse the name of the Lord your God, for the Lord will not hold anyone guiltless who misuses his name.

"Observe the Sabbath day by keeping it holy, as the Lord your God has commanded you. Six days you shall labor and do all your work, but the seventh day is a Sabbath to the Lord your God. On it you shall not do any work, neither you, nor your son or daughter, nor your manservant or maidservant, nor your ox, your donkey or any of your animals, nor the alien within your gates, so that your manservant and maidservant may rest, as you do. Remember that you were slaves in Egypt and that the Lord your God brought you out of there with a mighty hand and an outstretched arm. Therefore the Lord your God has commanded you to observe the Sabbath day.

"Honor your father and your mother, as the Lord your God has commanded you, so that you may live long and that it may go well with you in the land the Lord your God is giving you.

"You shall not murder,

"You shall not commit adultery,

"You shall not steal,

"you shall not give false testimony against your neighbor, "You shall not covet your neighbors wife. You shall not set your desire on your neighbors house or land, his manservant or maidservant, his ox or donkey, or anything that belongs to your neighbor."

These are the commandments the Lord proclaimed in a loud voice to your whole assembly there on the mountain from out of the fire, the cloud and the deep darkness; and he added nothing more. Then he wrote them on two stone tablets and gave them to me.

Praise the Lord and repent you sinners! Yes some people repent and go and sin no more. You can do this if you are filled with the power of the Holy Spirit. Stay in the word of God and build up your spirit man—or spirit woman. Sin was associated with sickness. Like if you were hating on someone, then you would be the physically ill one. People in the jail want healed and I was fortunate enough to meet a person who had the gift of healing. He told me that when he was a young man, a dog came over to him with a broken leg and he touched it and it healed instantly. Now I believe

God can work through people if you are a submitted vessel to the Holy Spirit. It is God who heals—and He can work through you. Now if you hold anger to another, it will hinder the process, and if there are others nearby who have disbelief of Gods' healing power. So, he and I took a lap around the yard. He didn't physically touch my back but he grabbed the pain and drew it out and threw it away. Praise the Lord. I know I felt the pain leave, then my slight doubt was there and some small pain remained.

Matthew 9:27-30. As Jesus went on from there, two blind men followed him, calling out, "Have mercy on us, Son of David!" When he had gone indoors, the blind men came to him, and he asked them, "Do you believe that I am able to do this?" "Yes Lord", they replied. Then he touched their eyes and said, "According to your faith will it be done to you"; and their sight was restored.

In Jesus' hometown, he didn't do many miracles there because of the peoples' unbelief. See Matthew 13:53-58. This is why you have to believe in HIM! Being able to live a life with a forgiving spirit is healthy. Remember, the Lord said, "With forgiving, you'll be a living sanctuary for me." You have to forgive. Remember if you hold anger, you'll miss the blessing that is right in front of you. Some people look at jail as a spiritual retreat, and a place to learn things that you never knew. Jesus can save your health, save your life, and ultimately save your SOUL. Remember our topic of SOUL DIRECTION—you young juvenile delinquent criminal type reading now? The devil only uses you for evil, if you let him. Devil—evil. We all need to stay in the word of God. He is the vine and we are the branches.

John 15:1-8. "I am the true vine, and my Father is the gardener. He cuts off every branch in me that bears no fruit, while every branch that does bear fruit he prunes so that it will be even more fruitful. You are already clean because of the word I have spoken to you. Remain in me and I will remain in you. No branch can bear fruit by itself; it must remain in the vine. Neither can you bear fruit unless you remain in me.

"I am the vine; you are the branches. If a man remains in me and I in him, he will bear much fruit; apart from me you can do nothing. If anyone does not remain in me, he is like a branch that is thrown away and withers; such branches are picked up, thrown into the fire and burned. If you remain in me and my words remain in you, ask whatever you wish and it will be given you. This is to my father's glory, that you bear much fruit, showing yourselves to be my disciples.

We see the importance of staying in the word of God. God will bless us for obeying His word. Be not just hearers of the word, but also DOERS! Turn to God and He will heal us, but remember that we need to do our part and believe. Believe to receive the blessings of God. The distraction is the world and the fleeting happiness of wealth. I know some very wealthy people and they are completely miserable because they forgot about God, don't know God or are too distracted by the flesh. Everyone has a personal battle of the spirit vs. the flesh. The spirit wants what is contrary to the flesh and they war against each other. For I have been crucified with Christ, I no longer live, but Christ lives in me. All things have become new.

This is one problem with the legal system—they live in the past, looking at you for the murder that you did back in 1970. Well, you are not the same person that you were, especially if God has made you a new person. But when they look at you, it is 1970. I once heard that losers live in the past and winners live in the future. What matters is NOW and the future. Live in the love of God and be a peaceful presence. Only the devil wants you to kill, steal and destroy.

Give him an inch and he will take your life. Resist the devil and he will flee from you. Claim the blood of Jesus—say it out loud. "Get thee behind me satan, even you will worship the true and living God, as it is written." The man at yard who God used as a tool to heal me, he says this when evil spirits or influences are around.

For example: One time when I was at yard, a man with multiple personality disorder—by my own diagnosis—was far ahead of me out of auditory (hearing) range. We know it wasn't HE who committed whatever crime, but one of the personalities living in him. Anyway, I know evil when I see it, and I started saying quietly; "I cast you out in the name of Jesus Christ!" No way he could have heard me. Well he turned around—and he was far away—and all I heard was him yelling as loud as he could, "You no good mf'er! Leave us alone!" He was a small skinny guy but if he has a demon in him, superhuman strength is possible. Remember the importance of lifting weights-BIG DOG? Medical science only believes what they can see or touch. Jesus knows about demon possession because He drove out demons. Now are you gonna say that demons are not real? Jesus only tells the TRUTH. He is the Truth, the Way and the Life. He is the only way to God The FATHER. I hope this is all exciting for you also!

Being a Christian means holding a higher standard. You and your lifestyle might be the only bible that a person reads, so act appropriately. Tell the truth. Look what happened to me from a lie, but God will judge them for bearing false witness. He will take revenge. God can turn a horrible tragedy—my jail time—into a beautiful testimony.

OK, things people do in jail;

Get beat up—Yes people get beat up in jail. I never did 'cause I lifted weights and had Sammy and Afro and I knew how to talk to people and respect everyone. The most dangerous people were my friends. I'd just go and start talking to them all. Big Scary—we will call him—was one of my weight lifting partners. He could bench 300 lbs. easy. He was too strong for his own good. People would say, "Why you give him a hand shake and hug? He's a dangerous man!" Those were my friends because The Lord blessed me with communication skills.

The one new CO got beat up. He came to the jail with the rah-rah, and the "I got the badge" attitude and his mouth got his butt kicked. All over someone passed a cigarette through the center yard fence. He didn't talk to them RESPECTFULLY about it. They don't break up fights, they let you tire yourself out until you can't breathe, then you are done.

Proverbs 13:3. He who guards his lips guards his life, but he who speaks rashly will come to ruin.

Another prisoner got beat up in the chow hall line. It was spaghetti day as we who remember can testify to the truth. Two prisoners in the lunch line were punching each other and a third prisoner was stuck in between them, so he got punched too. The one who lost the fight was standing there with his two hands under his chin catching all of his blood that was running out of his face, and we were all wondering what he was gonna do with the blood. TRAUMA! Then the big white hat mountain guy CO came over and grabbed the "winner"—if we can call him that—and he got some new shiny bracelets to wear. Handcuffs. White hat is a Lieutenant. I hope rethinking my trauma is helping you—you young juvenile delinquent criminal type. Then if you fight, and a guard—CO—see's you, you get 30 days in the hole. 3 showers a week and 23 hours a day locked in your cell. Self control is a fruit of the spirit.

Galatians 5:16-26. So I say, live by the spirit, and you will not gratify the desires of the sinful nature. For the sinful nature desires what is contrary to the Spirit, and the Spirit what is contrary to the sinful nature. They are in conflict with each other, so that you do not do what you want. But if you are led by the Spirit, you are not under law.

The acts of the sinful nature are obvious: sexual immorality, impurity and debauchery; idolatry and witchcraft; hatred, discord, jealousy, fits of rage, selfish ambition, dissensions, factions and envy; drunkenness, orgies, and the like. I warn you, as I did before, that those who live like this will not inherit the kingdom of God.

But the fruit of the Spirit is love, joy, peace, patience, kindness, goodness, faithfulness, gentleness and self-control. Against such things there is no law. Those who belong to Christ Jesus have crucified the sinful nature with its passions and desires. Since we live by the Spirit, let us keep in step with the Spirit. Let us not become conceited, provoking and envying each other.

So I'm here doing one of my jobs which is typing up all of this to hopefully turn a soul from death row, to hopefully save the life of a police officer, and to keep the young juvenile informed that God is very real, and only Jesus Christ can save your soul from hell.

The phone rings and it is my dad telling me that the things he said that I could have to take for junk runs, well he is giving stuff to one of his friends to sell at the flea market. May today-July 13, 2011—live in this book forever as a testimony of Jesus Christ. You see, you can know the bible and how to react biblically to things that happen in every day life. How would Jesus react to what just happened to me? So I go over to dads and start helping them load up all of these things in the guys van—the things that I was supposed to take to the junk yard and get money to pay my truck insurance which is due now. Needless to say, I started telling everyone what was on my mind.

James 3:5-8. Likewise the tongue is a small part of the body, but it makes great boasts. Consider what a great forest is set on fire by a small spark. The tongue also is a fire, a world of evil among the parts of the body. It corrupts the whole person, sets the whole course of his life on fire, and is itself set on fire by hell.

All kinds of animals, birds, reptiles and creatures of the sea are being tamed and have been tamed by man, but no man can tame the tongue. It is a restless evil, full of deadly poison.

Perhaps my tongue said a few things it should not have said. Dad has memory loss and didn't remember that he gave me the stuff. I carried the junk to the guys van telling him it was MY stuff and dad forgot that he said so. I needed to pay the 200 for my insurance!

You're taking my stuff! I was MAD. Then I told them all this is, is just a distraction from my MAIN PURPOSE of typing up this book! It doesn't matter. It is more blessed to give than receive and may the Lord bless dad for giving his things away. Give and it will be given to you. I took the case to the Lord and explained that I need money for bills! Forget about that junk, we got bigger fish to fry—KEEP TYPING TONY! Have I not always provided for you? Sammy taught me that you have to let things go because there will be more B.S. coming.

Where were we? People in the jail doing things.

"Want to earn a jolly rancher?"—If someone asks you to take their ice cream tickets and run to the yard like a nut to the ice cream stand—to beat the line—for them, then you deserve a jolly rancher.

Biggest food waste I have ever seen—Many, many people throw away their oranges, apples, bananas, cereal, toast, milk, juice, etc . . . then some of them wonder why they are not healthy. At least offer it to someone at your table. Chances are, someone will accept the food! Most commissaries have vitamins you can buy on your one day a week shopping visit. When I left, you would fill out your store order and put it on your door at night and then it was only a two week wait until you got your stuff. So you would sit and think, "What am I gonna need two weeks from now?"

Water restrictions—When I left, they were putting water controls on the sinks and toilets. Less flushes, less water, more stress.

Breathe through your mouth—not your nose—The room was 8 feet by 8 feet. If you have a nasty smell that comes from your butt, sit on the toilet and give a courtesy flush! Air also gets sucked down the toilet. Even a cat can sit on the toilet and flush. Do to others as you would have them do to you. My one celly would stink so bad, that a guy came in our cell yelling at him about it. It's not always funny to rip one then look around and say, "Is everyone all right?"

Three day lock down—Three or four times a year you get to be locked in your cell with your celly for THREE DAYS. Hope you don't have claustrophobia. Then the guards or the CERT teams come in and do the strip search—oh I forgot—after they make you spread your butt cheeks so they can look up there, then you turn around and have to lift up your penis so they can look at your scrotum. After all, there might be a weapon under there. This is why your mind makes you forget all these terrible things they do to you. This is why people get out and get a gun and remember—the only one standing at the sidelines is the devil. Got Jesus in your life? Sure is lucky for all of them that I do. So they come in your cell and put all of your stuff on your cellys bed and vice versa. They march around the jail with their black plastic outfits on and we would laugh at them and call them names out of our windows. "Look! there's the fat Sarge! How did he squeeze into that plastic outfit?" Keep your eyes on the Lord and forget all of the evil they did to you for a crime you were not guilty of. I don't think it is healthy for me to rethink all of this but if it saves you or someone else from jail, then it is worth it. Three days with no shower, fed through a hole in the door. Hope it's not 90 degrees out.

Coffee addicts—People that you don't even know come to the door with a cup in their hand and request for you to help feed their flesh. Also high request items are creamer, sugar, cigarettes, a light, snacks, toilet paper—they could just use a sock like I had to, you know? Things requested from friends, acquaintances, and people you have not seen before.

"Don't let nobody con you!" My dad would say this to me while I was there. Some people try to get all they can from you. They will rob your cell if they can. Two guys went in the one guy's cell to rob him and all they took was an ass kicking. The security guy says that they got what they deserved, no charges filed.

Pray before the shower—There is a room with at least 20 shower heads along 2 walls and you all stand around in your white boxer shorts and take a shower. Sometimes it would be crowded and you would splash the person next to you and vice versa. Then people have their friends save them a shower by putting a wash rag above the shower head. I saw a guy get punched in the head when a guy asked him for the end shower and he didn't say the right thing out of his mouth.

Proverbs 15:1 A gentle answer turns away wrath, but a harsh word stirs up anger.

Inmate vs. staff—It is best not to say any more than you have to—to these people. Sure, be polite and respectful, but they don't want to hear about all of the things your celly does. That is what the psychologists and psychiatrists get paid for. If you have a real emergency, go to the Sarge or a white hat-(Lieutenant). Remember that crap flows downhill, not up. One

C.O.—Correction Officer—informed me that he would always get in trouble for not writing up enough people. So they look for trouble and produce trouble-sometimes—if there is none. Same as a cop has to have so many tickets or they get in trouble from their boss. So stay out of the way for your own benefit. The bible says to obey those who are in authority.

Romans 13:1-7. Everyone must submit himself to the governing authorities, for there is no authority except that which God has established. The authorities that exist have been established by God. Consequently, he who rebels against the authority is rebelling against what God has instituted, and those who do so will bring judgment on themselves. For rulers hold no terror for those who do right, but for those who do wrong. Do you want to be free from fear of the one in authority? Then do what is right and he will commend you. For he is God's servant to do you good. But if you do wrong, be afraid, for he does not bear the sword for nothing. He is God's servant, an agent of wrath to bring punishment on the wrongdoer. Therefore, it is necessary to submit to the authorities, not only because of possible punishment but also because of conscience. This is also why you pay taxes, for the authorities are God's servants, who give their full time to governing. Give everyone what you owe him: If you owe taxes, pay taxes; if revenue, then revenue; if respect, then respect; if honor, then honor.

People struggle with these topics because the one magistrate went to jail for whatever charge he had. Cops go to jail. Politicians go to jail, and many innocent people go to jail. Before my trial happened, fifty thousand dollars cash—of borrowed money that I have to pay back—changed hands. I thought it was steep for a payoff and I wondered why do I have to pay ANYTHING? WHEN?I'M?NOT?GUILTY? I was informed that they find you guilty with no DNA evidence. In my case, there was no proof, no DNA. Due to the high cost of living, it was fifty grand or see you in 50 years. Your choice. Well the one guy handling all this—he dies. So I go to his family and needed the money to do this myself and his family dummys up real quick, but I see a new roof going on their house—and mine is currently falling off—I see a new dirtbike in the yard, and everyone had the I have a lot of money glow to them. Reason for murder? Reason to forgive. Now I'll be treated like a normal poor citizen—guilty. No more celebrity status payoff and walk free for me. Sad but true, but this is how it is. I can't hear you unless you are handing me money. What did you say? Who's his lawyer? How much cash they got? It's all a mystery. Now they are really pissed off, because we all have a do list and a money list and their money list is now 50 grand less. Now we get a new lawyer and try to see if the system works. It don't. We beat 40 years and I get the other 10 years-8 in jail and 2 on probation. Probably because a small bit of that money did trinckle in somewhere at the beginning. Reason to forgive. So you just keep believing that no one lies, no one pays off anyone, and innocent people don't go to jail. I believe the Lord was watching all of us and just shaking his head in disgust. This is why people kill and I forgive. God will judge even the judges, and just imagine the thunder that God might have in His courtroom on their judgment day. God appointed them, as the bible says, and there is no payoff in heaven. Maybe this is what this book should be called? NO PAYOFF IN HEAVEN. Now don't steal it 'cause I already own the copyrights. Once again, you have to buy that! Now would you be mad if you were me? Only if you are human.

So believe me when I tell you that I have been bothered enough by these people. I should be a doctor now as I was making A's in college, but now I'm an author, greenhouser, junk runner!, and a preacher—at least to my own family and friends. Maybe in five years, I'll have money from those cactus seeds that I ordered from Arizona? Sure, it would be nice to make money from this book—I hope that I do—to help my family, but what is most important is that God's Word is marching forward. His kingdom is advancing against the strongholds of evil. If the soul of someone is helped to be redirected from the fire of hell, then all of my loss was for eternal gain.

Shakedown on the block—If a resident see's them approaching the block, someone yells this, and I would yell it to—"shakedown on the block!". Two guards walking in with a metal clip board with trashing your cell on their mind. People hide their gambling tickets, etc . . . If there are two of you in a cell, one will leave, 'cause they can only search your cell if you are both there, unless it is an investigative search. One time my celly and I were at yard and we returned and a tornado went through our cell. An investigative search happened. Nothing was found, but you still have to clean up the mess they make, and there's no apology, just like when they let you out of jail. That is why this book exists—something good HAS TO come out of all of this destruction of Tony. The person that you were when you went to jail, well that person died. They killed that person. You become a new, hopefully better person, and trust God to give you a new life and since you lost your wife, your dog, family, house, car, dirtbike, quad, truck, job, everything, God really is all that you have left. He will not leave you nor forsake you. When God is all you have, you will find that God is all you need.

Noise levels—I was born and raised in a quiet neighborhood. Myself and a few others there have determined that the noisiest residents are the Puerto Ricans, then the blacks, then the whites. Asian people are quiet also. This is just how it is, after careful consideration.

Yelling on the PA system—Public address system should be used with respect, but—"YOU IN THE JAIL!" The one Sarge yells on the PA and calls people rude names and calls them on to fight him. Is—or was—this setting a good example for the prisoners? Was it helping to 'correct' anyone? No, but it's a perfect example of what I never want to be. Remember Jesus is our role model to follow. Do, say, and act as He would. Read all of the bible and what is in red letters. The red letters are what Jesus said. If everyone woke up, took their gos-pill (gospel), which is the good news of Jesus, the world would be a better place.

Mark 9:2-7. After six days Jesus took Peter, James and John with him and led them up a high mountain, where they were all alone. There he was transfigured before them. His clothes became dazzling white, whiter than anyone in the world could bleach them. And there appeared before them Elijah and Moses, who were talking with Jesus.

Peter said to Jesus, "Rabbi, it is good for us to be here. Let us put up three shelters—one for you, one for Moses and one for Elijah."(He did not know what to say, they were so frightened.)

Then a cloud appeared and enveloped them, and a voice came from the cloud: "This is my Son, whom I love. Listen to him!"

So I listen to Jesus. He is the only way that we can have better lives. Overcome evil with good. If you feed into evil when it comes at you, the evil escalates. Most murders start with an argument. Snuff it out at the beginning.

No cure for stupid—I would never call anyone stupid, because when I look at myself—BOY WAS I STUPID! For hanging around the wrong people, and putting yourself in a dumb predicament, you need to wise up! We all need to pray for God to bless us with wisdom, and pray everyday for God to guide you. Man or woman, they think they know how to do something, but when the Lord guides you, then you are better able to do the task at hand.

Proverbs 2:1-6. My son, if you accept my words and store up my commands within you, turning your ear to wisdom and applying your heart to understanding, and if you call out for insight and cry aloud for understanding, and if you look for it as for silver and search for it as for hidden treasure, then you will understand the fear of the Lord and find the knowledge of God. For the Lord gives wisdom, and from His mouth come knowledge and understanding.

We got somethin' to say, and it is the truth. Jesus would repeatedly say, "I tell you the truth . . ." We are always to tell the truth and a trial is to be a search for the truth. God created the earth and people, and all else. He cannot lie! That is something He cannot do. The devil is the father of lies. We have God with the truth and the devil with the lies, so who you gonna follow? You have to be armed with the word of God, because what I say—doesn't matter. What God says—matters. Now if someone speaks the Word of God, then I listen because we are all spirit deficient to a degree, and we need to fill up our spirit person with the Word of God. Be not just a hearer, but a doer, of God's Word.

Titus 1:2." . . . God, who does not lie . . ."

Numbers 23:19. God is not a man, that he should lie, . . .

Paradise missing—A few people that I knew of there, lost their testicles in a fight. One person had his bitten off. One guy got raped in the shower. So you see that you need to pray to God for safety while you are there. If you can lift weights, you should. My one friend there can bench 500 lbs. and no one bothers him. Jail is where you don't want to be.

Bird feeders—We're not supposed to feed the birds there, but we did. If you see a baby bird crying for food, I had to throw bread pieces, after all the bread was just going in the garbage with all of the other food. We had sparrows, starlings, grackles, pigeons, crows, and an occasional hawk. Yes, obey authority, but we had to feed the birds.

Got sleep?—You have to arrange your sleep or nap times around the four counts. They make you stand up to be seen as they walk around-6 am, 1 pm, 6 pm, and 9 pm. Then they shine flashlights on you in the night to see if you are in your bed. I would try to sleep from 9:30 pm to 5:30 am. A day time nap around noon also seems to be beneficial, especially if you work and are on an indoor weight lifting program. You need proper rest to deal with the stresses associated with the place and the people. The only places you go are to the library, indoor gym, chow hall, church, education building, yard, blockout. A real nut show. When's it end? When you walk out that front gate. Just retyping all of this, causes stress and brings vivid memories—post trauma. I told God, a few days ago—"I'm done! The book is over!" My family see's a noticeable difference as this book takes away some of my peace. A lot of people would get out of jail, then months or years later would be right there walking up the sidewalk again. Back for more B.S. So I relate my current book anxiety to being a personal crime deterrent method. Just a slight memory so you don't spit on the sidewalk. People forget how it was and then they slip back to jail. The Lord says something to the effect of; KEEP TYPING TONY! Your pain is my gain. So my pain of authoring this, is to the Lords' GLORY. Praise the Lord. Sleep is needed and I would often dream a dream of home in a bed ALONE with no celly in the room. Take a walk in the woods or order a large pizza? You take it for granted unless you have been stolen away. They take your body but your mind is free. The Lord is your comfort, so pray for a good nights sleep.

CHAPTER 5

Preparing for Release

Luke 8:39 "Return home and tell how much God has done for you."

While you are in the jail, you can look into different trades to learn. Get your GED if you need it. Take a college class if offered. Get a job while you are there so you at least have some money so you don't have to go door to door asking for things, like so many do. 75 cents is a matter of life or death in the jail. Dealing with all of the people is a great lesson of how to communicate more efficiently in a multicultural society. Paul knew how to talk to many different people as we see him in the book of Acts. Sharpen your communication skills in the man made hell of jail.

God wants us to fellowship and spread the good news of Jesus. Tell someone of how God healed you or did a miracle in your life. Christian friends are good to have and a lot of people wanted a celly who was about Gods' business.

If you have a job there, it can help you develop workplace skills such as being on time, having a positive attitude, working well with others, being a good example by having respectable conduct, and performing different job skills.

As an example, I took welding classes and have become a nationally certified welder. The schooling was fun and it was rough to study with all of the noise, but God helped us to make it. Most of us passed, and we had a great teacher. You get out of it what you put into it, as far as your final grade is concerned. So learn a trade and then you won't have to sling crack on the street corners! Those things lead to jail.

At the start of Rockview, I got drafted into the kitchen and had to wipe tables at the chow hall, then passed out food on the meal line, then washed pans in the pan room, then they made me a cook. So I gained 30 pounds and lifted weights. Then, I had to get out of that nut house kitchen. So, I took my Deans List certificate and went to see the principal—after they wrote me a pass to do so. "Deans List! We need you!", the principal said. He took me in to a class room and introduced me to a staff teacher and I started the next day. So, I taught school for 6 years. Reading groups were my favorite. Let's help each other read. I had to do class lessons and get up in front of everyone and write word problems on the chalk board, had new students, etc. "Mr. Morich, your 9:30 student is here—Mr. Smith . . ." So I had people coming at me all day long. One time, one of the prisoner teachers went to the hole, so we other teachers had 50 students each day. I'd just teach 2 at a time, by Gods' grace. The welding school was after the 6+ years of teaching. I had to do something for me before I got out. Then, the insane welding crew job was next. My hands on experience was happening. Everyone got hurt, it was the nature of the job. You learned real quick to watch all around you.

So do something for you and help someone while you are there. The devil has stolen enough and he is stealing no more. We are armed with the Spirit of God—The Holy Spirit.

We need to know who The Holy Spirit is. God the Father, God the Son, God the Holy Spirit. The mantra of our class room was repetition. You need to repeat things for people because—1.They didn't hear you the first time, 2.If you hear things one time, you might forget it. 3. Repeating it, drives it home. God is One God, three persons. God the Father sent Jesus—God the Son—To die on the cross for our sins, to destroy the work of the devil. Jesus laid down his life, no one took it from him. Jesus died, was buried, rose again, was seen by His disciples, and went back to heaven. Jesus sent the Holy Spirit to be our helper. Jesus will return again someday—only God the Father knows when this will happen. This is all in the bible and I just quickly summarized it for those who need to know the truth.

Genesis 1:26 Then God said, "Let us make man in our image, . . ."

Matthew 26:52 "Put your sword back in its place," Jesus said to him, "for all who draw the sword will die by the sword. Do you think I cannot call on my Father, and he will at once put at my disposal more than twelve legions of angels? But how then would the Scriptures be fulfilled that say it must happen in this way?"

John 19:30 When he had received the drink, Jesus said, "It is finished." With that, he bowed his head and gave up his spirit.

Acts 1:6-11 So when they met together, they asked him, "Lord, are you at this time going to restore the kingdom to Israel?"

He said to them: "It is not for you to know the times or dates the Father has set by his own authority. But you will receive power when the Holy Spirit comes on you; and you will be my witnesses in Jerusalem, and in all Judea and Samaria, and to the ends of the earth."

The same Spirit—The Holy Spirit—who conceived Jesus in Mary, rose Jesus from the dead, enabled miracles—Three in one God, this Spirit lives in all of us believers. We who are Christians and are submitted to God, we have The Holy Spirit helping us. Remember God sang to me; "With forgiving, you'll be a living sanctuary for me." When we forgive all of the years taken from us, God-The Holy Spirit—will live in us. I wouldn't say anything if it wasn't true. Only by Gods power are we able to speak about God, knowing that God will judge me someday for every word that I put in this book. His judgment is just and correct. Remember there is no payoff in heaven. I believe God will say something to the effect of, "What did you do with the life that I gave you?" He knit you together in your mothers' Womb.

This is CRIME PREVENTION and SOUL DIRECTION. Skip the life sentence or possible jail time, get a bible and read it, and get yourself in a good church to learn more about God and plant a money seed. God always blesses you when you put money at a church. God says to put Him to the test.

Malachi 3:10-12 "Bring the whole tithe into the storehouse, that there may be food in my house. Test me in this," says the Lord Almighty, "and see if I will not throw open the floodgates of heaven and pour out so much blessing that you will not have room enough for it. I will prevent pests from devouring your crops, and the vines in your fields will not cast their fruit," says the Lord Almighty. "Then all the nations will call you blessed, for yours will be a delightful land," says the Lord Almighty.

John 14:26-27 But the Counselor, the Holy Spirit, whom the Father will send in my name, will teach you all things and will remind you of everything I have said to you. Peace I leave with you; my peace I give you. I do not give to you as the world gives. Do not let your hearts be troubled and do not be afraid.

I know a few millionaires who are completely miserable because only God can give you the peace and happiness that you need. The money helps to pay the bills but you need God to have only the peace that God can give you.

The Lord is mighty to save. I keep feeling it and hearing it throughout this project book. We're preparing for release in case you are still in the jail. Have God in you life. Remember where you came from. That is what Scott told me at the yard right before exit stage right day. He said, "I'll take your place." Huh? "Wish I could take you with me.", I replied. "No, give me your ID and I'll tell them I'm Tony Morich and I'll go home and take care of mom and dad, and fix up the house." All I could say was it's not mine to give. We know that the Lord sets prisoners free. But I remember where I came from. Being in that big yard field up in the mountains, lifting weights and singing Jesus songs with Warner. He's a big strong guy who loves Jesus and he was in jail since 1975. I would hear people walking by and saying how the white man got me up on the mountain and he won't let me out. Then a black guy said that it was a black man who sent him there. On and on for years and years. You sit back and watch your family members die, your dog dies, your wife leaves-but not always. My girlfriend made it 8 months. One guy said his woman had all his stuff sold on the day he went to jail. I heard about every story from all of my different cellys. So you don't want to go back to jail once you do get out. One guy forgot about God and he went back to jail and was in our bible group telling us about it. The next chapter will also help to prepare you for going home. Excitement was waiting for me—good and bad, Lets walk out the front gate together, into freedom. You smell that? It's something you don't know nothing about—freedom.

Isaiah 54:16-17 "See, it is I who created the blacksmith who fans the coals into flame and forges a weapon fit for its work. And it is I who have created the destroyer to work havoc; no weapon forged against you will prevail, and you will refute every tongue that accuses you. This is the heritage of the servants of the Lord, and this is their vindication from me," declares the Lord.

CHAPTER 6

Finally Home

The gate opened, dad and Rich were there and we left. First on the agenda? No, not a woman, a Big-Mac! It was one good sandwich too. Then we had to go straight to the parole office, because I was free but I wasn't. Two years of probation. So we meet my supervisor and he's a big guy. We're all in his office talking and he says, "This is how we're gonna do this." He leans forward and pulls out his wallet and flips it open in front of me to show me his badge and asks me, "Does this mean anything to you!?" Well I only had a mini heart attack from that but I put my hands up and said yes sir. "What does it mean?", he asked. I replied, "It means you can say anything you want and people believe you." "Like what?", he asks. Anything. He looked sad for a second because he saw that this is what the law had done to me and meant to me. He saw that I was the model prisoner and no misconducts so two more years should be easy. I had to go to the everyone on probation/parole meeting. Was it 2 times a week for like 9 months? Job search, etc . . .

So after we met the parole/probation—it's the same thing, then I got to return home. 8 years later and things were different. A new library, stop-light, new stores, low rider cars with big mufflers hanging off the back end. We call them buzzbombs. Why do we have to dial the area code now? 4 dollars a gallon of gas? Are you nuts? All the greed in the world can't put it that high.

So I'm walking up the front steps of my mom and dads house and I'm carrying my one box and TV and no one told me about the new gap in the walk and I'm looking up at all of them waving to me and I trip and slide on my one knee and my arms and box and TV go crashing into the wall of the house. "Why didn't you have the camera ready for that one?", I asked.

After that, we all talked and it was time to see my house. Rich and I waiked over and we looked at how big the trees grew in 8 years. The little pine tree, which was never taller than me, was now 30 feet high. Those bastards!, I thought. That's a word I haven't used for a long time. So we look in the house and it needs work—to use a great understatement. I remember English class. Rockview is over now and the parole officer told me that I'm going through trauma! I guess so. Still am. Back to the house where I now sit typing with my guard dog chiauaua beagle terrior over on the couch.

So Rich tells me as we jump back to 1999, then 2007, "You know they broke in twice?" WHO WHAT and WHERE?

I calmly say, "They can come back-I got something for them. It's called 8 years of Rockview." I heard the cops didn't do nothing but would have if the issue was pursued, I'm sure. To serve and protect. I read a lot of the law books when I was there, and people simply do not know the laws. So the house and I lived through it all. A new beginning from an old ending. Trusting Jesus to provide and help put the pieces back together. One church lady penpal sent 200 dollars and I told mom, "See! someone really does care, and it comes from a person who is in the body of Christ." This church place sent me clothes. The Lord was very helpful.

My childhood friend since 1980—Rodney Smith—would fill up my old junk truck that the welfare place bought me! He would say, "Go get some money for you." I think he felt sorry for the devastated state you are dropped back into upon release. Now I'm blessed but always have on the armor of God.

Romans 7:13. "For if you live according to the sinful nature, you will die; but if by the Spirit you put to death the misdeeds of the body, you will live.

That sums it up completely. Temptation came, also the distractions of the world. The need for money, food, HEAT! Were did God go? I haven't heard his voice as much. Remember—draw near to him and he will draw near to you. Time went by—the probation drug on but I was free. To stand in the yard at night after 9 pm. No more in the cage for at least 12 hours a day. We had the curfew and pay them and pee in the bottle once a month at the monessen police station. How ya' doin', sir? bla bla bla whatever. Go through the motions, don't spit on the sidewalk, and obey the laws. Very nice people they all were. So I get a job—so I can have food to eat—you understand. This is for the young juvenile delinquent—this is still CRIME PREVENTION. If your mom and dad are rich and even if poor—if you bring some dumb charge on yourself, stupid for you. Then your parents with their 30 years to go at 2000 dollars a month—you get the picture? No one needs to go be dumb and go to jail, or to get out and rebuild your life, then go back.

That's why I don't do NOTHING to go back there.
I'd rather stay home and help the family. If you can
survive on cactus seeds and junk runs—good luck! A
lot of people do junk runs. Girls pull in the junkyard
with aluminum cans in their car trunks and cash in.
Just imagine—You can go to the dollar store down
town and do the dollar menu at the drive through.

Praise the Lord! I know people in jail who would
pay a million dollars to get out and you can keep the
charge. So a dollar menu was a complete luxury. Rich
people might be too good for a 89 cent hamburger,
but my dog Funny—who my next book is about,
loves just a little burger. Not much, 'cause she is on a
healthy good dog diet. It's all in the book.

People in jail say, "They can just let me out." So
if you are in the free world—the real world—as we
would call it, obey the laws and stay free.

So I get a good job and I'm doing 25 yards a day,
and I'm in better shape than when I was 20. Plus or
minus 25 yards. If Jesus is on the cover, you HAVE
to tell the truth. I was spraying yards like a mad man.
Brutal workout—ten miles a day walked—at least.

One day after work, I come home and up my
driveway—now I have an alarm and a camera—well,
I look over and my kitchen door is wide open and I
know I locked it. The devil was still busy behind the
scenes. My door is broke open, drawers open—didn't

this already happen twice when I was on vacation? What do I have that people want? I'm just a poor person going to work to pay the bills and live my life after a traumatic ordeal! So my dirtbike is gone out of my living room. Now somebodys getting their ass kicked. You don't mess with my bike, it's a very personal thing and anyone who rides or races will understand. I was so mad I couldn't talk. Dad said, "Call the cops!" Just what I wanted to do today. 911. Pockets inside out and everything. I went to every neighbors house and they all helped me. It's neighborhood watch. We won't say no names but the cops knew who it was. You can never slide the bible aside and let your anger get the best of you. I found my bike myself with Rich helping, police helping and God. God knows where everything is. I was way out in these woods and I would look up and yell, "Wheres my bike at?", to the Lord. Now we have cable locks on the 300 dollar quad.

The one police officer went with the Sarge and looked on their own time in the dark with flashlights. Those men are true professionals and went out of their way to help me. There are some really good police officers as two of my friends are police. Good and bad is everywhere in life. Remember the armor of God:

Ephesians 6:10-20. Finally, be strong in the Lord and in his mighty power. Put on the full armor of God so that you can take your stand against the devil's schemes. For our struggle is not against flesh and blood, but against the rulers, against the authorities, against the powers of this dark world and against the spiritual forces of evil in the heavenly realms. Therefore put on the full armor of God, so that when the day of evil comes, you may be able to stand your ground, and after you have done everything, to stand. Stand firm then, with the belt of truth buckled around your waist, with the breastplate of righteousness in place, and with your feet fitted with the readiness that comes from the gospel of peace. In addition to all this, take up the shield of faith, with which you can extinguish all the flaming arrows of the evil one. Take the helmet of salvation and the sword of the Spirit, which is the word of God. And pray in the spirit on all occasions with all kinds of prayers and requests. With this in mind, be alert and always keep on praying for all the saints.

Pray also for me, that whenever I open my mouth, words may be given me so that I will fearlessly make known the mystery of the gospel, for which I am an ambassador in chains. Pray that I may declare it fearlessly, as I should.

This brings us to a crossroad. Evil verses good. You have the choice to decide if you will do evil or good. Whose side are you on? The devil or the Lord is your choice. There are blessings for obedience to God and curses for disobedience. See in your bible—Deuteronomy chapter 28. You will be so blessed if you obey the Lord's commands and utterly destroyed if you disobey God.

Deuteronomy 30:15-18. See, I set before you today life and prosperity, death and destruction. For I command you today to love the Lord your God, to walk in his ways, and to keep his commands, decrees and law; then you will live and increase, and the Lord your God will bless you in the land you are entering to possess.

But if your heart turns away and you are not obedient, and if you are drawn away to bow down to other gods and worship them, I declare to you this day that you will certainly be destroyed.

Do you see the seriousness of obeying God? This book is a high calling on me to help people to learn to forgive, love your enemies, pray for those who persecute you, overcome evil with good, to NOT go and hurt any cops or judges when you do get out. Most disturbing to me was what I heard people say in the jail. One guy said that when he gets out, he was gonna kill the lawyer, the lawyers family, the dog, the cat, the bird, the goldfish, and all because he says he is not guilty of his charge. That's why he is gonna live through the jail for another 15 years to do this when he gets out. I would tell him to forgive. One guy said he will get his AK-47 out when he gets home and show them that he is in control. Sounds like the devil has control of him. Remember that demons are very real. Live the love of Jesus. This is what Warner told me. I asked him to tell me one thing as I was going home. LIVE THE LOVE OF JESUS. I wish everyone did this. Wake up, read your bible for soul instruction, be kind to others. Remember the fruit of the spirit? Love, joy, peace, patience, faithfulness, goodness, kindness, gentleness, self-control? Against such things there is no law. No law against you if you show or do an act of kindness, show gentleness, be nice or polite to someone. You get the picture?

"You should be a preacher, Tony.", my family tells me. At least in this book, I am. This leads us to a very exciting story that I would like to share with you. If you are in the jail reading this, the story coming up will be your great escape-at least a mental escape. All the names have been changed to protect the guilty and the innocent involved. Remember, I own the movie rights too, so you have to pay me off to get the whole story.

The date is May 14, 1965. Tom and Velma are in the middle of a field that this newly-wed couple have just purchased. Sweat is running down his face—as was a daily event for him—as he is digging a hole in the ground. "This is where the first pole will be put in the ground.", he says with a smile as he looks at his beautiful wife. She is pregnant and he has to work at the local mill to provide for his new family. She brings him an iced tea and gently wipes the sweat off of his face with the back of her hand. "This is why I love you, honey.", she says to him. He replies, "I have to get out of that mill! I can't take breathing all of the dirt, dust, and that mean boss—if he wasn't the boss . . ." She calmly replies, "Remember the Lord—He is mighty to save. When I was little, we had to use catalog pages for toilet paper!"

Their old truck is there with them and he puts the shovel in the back. Another day of surviving, is over. Life was more simple back then. Everyone left their doors open at night, there was no pain pill addictions, no crazy laws like we have today. The greed and money problems existed but in a different way. Jesus was there with our young newly-wed couple named—Tom and Velma.

Years go by and their new business was established with blood, sweat and tears. Fast Joey was hired to help run the show. He was very young at the time. Fast Joey hired me to help him. "Why can't you be like Tony?, he shows up early-leaves when he wants to—knows what needs to be done, I don't even have to see him at all to lead him around.", Joey would tell the other workers. I would come and go and Joey would always ask me, "When you coming back?" So I would go and help out. More years go by.

Then the call came, a terrible accident occurred and Tom was accidentally killed. Velma was a grieving widow, and Joey was to run the million dollar business for Velma, and I was helping Joey. Now Joey never knew of God and he was more focused on the flesh and the pleasures thereof. This gave the devil a foothold. Give him an inch and he will be your ruler. The cops came after Joey due to complaints from area citizens. Drugs, prostitution, embezzlement, and worse—were the charges. Joey called Velma and they were all in the office at the million+ dollar business with the cops and arresting officer present. "I'm sure we can work this out", was the theme of the room. A few cops were asked to leave and the cop in charge remained—The arresting officer. Velma was afraid as her husband was long gone and she knew that the cops were able to run her bank account and see that she had 47 million dollars. The officer says, "This can all go away—you know?" Fast Joey glances at Velma and then at the cop and says, "How much is this going to cost?" The cop gets that smirk on his face, and replies with seriousness, "5 million dollars."

Velmas' jaw hit the floor and she started to cry. Joey says, "5 million?" The money was paid with a special extra gift of a bobcat and a custom Harley. Joey avoided life in prison, and Velma went back home. The cops slowly took over the business as their new unofficial hangout. Joey would tell me, "I don't care if your head falls off and rolls away—you don't knock on my door for nothing—for the next hour." That kilo of coke was sure tasty—or so I was told. Sorry I just made that part up to add to the excitement of the book. Anyway! Shall we continue?

Years go by—Fast Joey beat the system and he was right at home all day barking out orders to his employees. "When you coming back?", he would ask me again. So I returned. One of the girls working there told me, "You know they made Joey the police commissioner?" I laughed so hard that I cried. I went down to see Joey alone. "Whats this I hear that YOU are the POLICE now, Joey!", I said laughing. "That's right!", he said. I told Joey, "Shut up and give me some money—POLICE MAN!" Joey asks me, "How much you need?"

Velma saw all of what happened to the business. She lost control of what her husband built. She would walk in and the cops were on the front porch or hanging out in the office. They would look at her and not see a person, they would see the millions of dollars. They would disrespect her on her own property, with a fake smile and a resentful nod. Until one day, she decided to take back what was hers. She woke up and seeked the Lords' guidance. "Guide me Lord!", she said as she opened her bible. She looked where she opened it to and it said; Genesis 19:24-25. Then the Lord rained down burning sulfur on Sodom and Gomorrah—from the Lord out of the heavens. Thus he overthrew those cities and the entire plain, including all those living in the cities—and also the vegetation in the land.

Velma got in her Mercedes and went to her business and told Joey, "I have something special planned for today." She smiled at him and with her eyes full of tears, her words were small but powerful. She said, "Do you remember Tom?" "Oh yes." Joey replied. "Tom was my husband and he built this all from an open field and I'm taking it back to an open field. I'm your boss Joey and you—starting this moment—will put everything, every single item on sale for half price."

Joey started to stutter, "But-but you can't just . . ." "Can't just what? I just did.", she said. "You have two weeks, then the bulldozers are coming to push over my buildings and any unsold merchandise." I never thought Joey could cry but he put his head down into his hands and cried so loud that others heard him, and Velma looked at him and said, "The Lord giveth and the Lord taketh away, blessed be the name of the Lord."

As she promised, in two weeks to the day, big trucks arrived and the big dozers started their engines. Joey stood at the front porch of the business looking out at them. Velma walked over to Joey and said, "You can go home now, we are finished." He didn't say a word as he got in his truck and left. The demolition took many weeks and the price was high—300,000 dollars cash. She didn't mind paying it at all. After it was all a field again, she drove to the front gate-only she has the key now—and walked out into the field where our story began. She smiled as she remembered gently wiping his sweat from his forehead on that day many years ago. She misses Tom but knows that he is in heaven waiting for her. Another tear runs down her cheek as she says quietly, "Now it's our place again, Tom."

Hope you liked the story! Sad part is that it is all true! Fast Joey went into exile in a different state, and there is a new commissioner who is doing the same as it always was. Why change things now? Millions of dollars to stay free. Mine was 50 grand and they didn't do what they were supposed to do. I gave it all to the Lord. If I never went to jail, this book would not exist. God's word always prevails.

Where were we? Finally home—to all of the peace, joy and happiness. My worse day out here is better than my best day in there. The Lord is MIGHTY to save. God continually provides on a daily basis. We must die daily by crucifying the flesh. With Gods' power, you can do this. The misdeeds of the flesh are to be put behind you and a new life in Christ is to be started. Then you need to be careful not to backslide into your old life. Support from other family members and Christian friends is helpful. Keep that focus on God and filter out the distractions of life which come at you daily. You have to work and get money, but be sure to include God in your plan.

On my one job, an older lady gave me a tip of a dollar bill and a can of pepsi. I was very grateful and appreciative BECAUSE there was a time when I couldn't drink a can of pop and I know people in jail understand it. You take for granted, the things you have everyday. To be able to be with a woman. People in most jails can't do that. To go in the woods for a walk, is what people miss while in jail. Who likes to ride quads? Aint no quads in the jail, Home. I would walk the yard alone and picture in my mind that I was riding a nice dirtbike. When I got home, I ended up getting the same bike by accident. God saw me at the jail mentally riding that bike and I ended up with it. There is a law—if you can call it that—what you continually take into your mind, you attract to you. It always happens this way. That's why kids playing those violent games is not beneficial. A bible tape is nice to listen to you. Someone reading the bible to you—what could be better? Everyone struggles—if you are human—with the desires of the flesh. Remember the flesh profits nothing, the Spirit gives life. Since we are a spirit in a body, then the two are in conflict. Just like heaven and hell, two opposing forces. The fire of hell is very real. This is that crossroads that we talked about before. You have the free will to choose between doing good or evil. It is your choice of heaven or hell. I personally hope that the whole world would do good and that people help each other. Life is rough enough! I would help the neighbor girl shovel her drive in the winter. I say this for God's Glory because whatever you do, do it as you are doing it for the Lord. Help somebody, just like Sammy Belle helped me. Afro helped me—Allen Williams—I see you on the sidewalk holding up this book in the air calling out to Sammy. Lord help us all. Sometimes He is the only one who can.

O.K. For legal reasons, I have to say that I made up some of this book. We gotta rap it up and move on to the next book. Jesus Christ is real and The Holy Spirit and God the Father. I hear people say the name, "Jesus", and they might use his name wrongly and I say, "Hey, that's the guy that saved me!" You have to speak up for the Lord. God helps me so much. Sure I need money to fix the house, help the family, etc . . . God helps those who help themselves. When you are doing a project or working towards a goal and things just start to come together, that is God helping out. God brings the people and things to you that you need. He is a present help in time of need.

We had a profit at our church. Gods power worked through this man to heal and to destroy the foot holds of the devil. An older lady was Spirit struck and laying on the floor, then when she was starting to get up, I helped her up and I felt the power of God going into my body from her. All tingly like and powerful, and it is only by Gods grace that I can rethink these book jail topics. I have to put it behind me and move on. Focus on the future and a better time. If you are in jail, keep on with the struggle. Sammy calls it as it is—a struggle. To fight this system that has you bound up. The Lord sets prisoners free. Sammy tells me that he keeps laying down and keeps waking up. The Lord is MIGHTY to save.

Your thoughts help to bring about the environment that surrounds you. So think about Jesus Christ. His sacrifice—it was once and it was for all.

Zephaniah 3:17 "The Lord your God is with you, he is mighty to save. He will take great delight in you, he will quiet you with his love, he will rejoice over you with singing."

I personally can testify about the truth and validity of these words. On May 30, 2004, God sang to me. It was between sleep and waking when my mind was more perceptive—for those of you who are scientific minded. "They say that Joseph was the favorite of Israel." That's what God said to me. I consulted my one lifer friend and we investigated more into what God was telling us.

Genesis 37:3 "Now Israel loved Joseph more than any of his other sons, because he had been born to him in his old age; and he made a richly ornamented robe for him."

In Genesis chapter 39, we see that Potiphars wife wanted Joseph to be with her and Joseph refused.

She lied and had Joseph put in jail. But the Lord was with Joseph while in prison. Joseph ended up being a great ruler because he obeyed God and the Spirit of God was very active in Josephs life. God can take a great tragedy and turn it into a great Victory for the Kingdom. The Kingdom of God advances forward breaking the strongholds of evil. The devil knows he is beat. I told him myself, "I belong to Jesus Christ now." You should have seen his face! So don't tell me about behavior. It is only God who can make you more powerful than Satan. Die daily, crucify the flesh, keep filled up with the scriptures and pray for an indwelling of the Holy Spirit. Invite the Holy Spirit into your life. God set me here and said, "TYPE!" And I hate to type. To be honest with you, I'm here typing and if I think about moving from the computer, I get dizzy and nauxious! I'm not saying that God is torturing me, I'm saying that He needs this book done and I'm fighting this process! Mercy Lord! "Jesus is near, we gonna make it!" God DOES rejoice over you with singing. You need positive peer support when you do get out. God said other things to me also which I will share with you.

I thought that I was either going nuts in the jail or that God really does talk or sing to people. I thought that people were nuts when they would say about God talking to them. I have to testify about the truth and that God is real. Only a fool says that there is no God.It doesn't matter if you hate or love me! What matters is that JESUS is being preached. God drew near to me because I drew near to Him. All I did mostly were bible studies, certificates, bible groups, etc . . . I had to find out who God was and why would He allow me to suffer in a prison? The Lord sends people to help you. I was on complete fire for the Lord. Burning desire for Jesus Christ. You should smile when you read that. Who is Jesus Christ? So the Lord answered me and He was very much in my ear or whatever the part of the body is that really hears things. For me His voice was like thunder, and angels would minister to me also. Others reading now who are very spiritual will understand. I heard things that even kings didn't hear.

Job 36:15. But those who suffer he delivers in their suffering; he speaks to them in their affliction.

Job 40:9. Do you have an arm like God's, and can your voice thunder like his?

Revelation 3:16-17. So, because you are lukewarm—neither hot nor cold—I am about to spit you out of my mouth. You say, 'I am rich; I have acquired wealth and do not need a thing.' But you do not realize that you are wretched, pitiful, poor, blind and naked.

Wow; wretched, pitiful, poor, blind, and naked. I believe that if you have all the money and don't know Jesus, then you are as He has said. Better to be poor like me yet extremely wealthy in faith. Don't get me wrong—I need all the help I can get! You reach a higher level of humanity when you submit to the Holy Spirit. You might not want to submit to the DOC, well submit to the Holy Spirit. He helps you always. You there reading—He is there and He is here with me as I type. Renew your mind. Scatzy—God rest his soul—would always tell me; 'Brother Tone, you just need a mental enema!' I'd say, "Yeah, just get out the big eraser and erase it all out of your mind." THEN—Renew your mind. Fill it up with BIBLE VERSES. I understand that churches are tax exempt. Someone must think they are doing something right! Gods LAWS always work. His laws do not change. I'm scared to death of hell, 'cause I know it is a real place. Then you are called to do the right thing and keep on doing the right thing. LIVE THE LOVE OF JESUS—remember? There is no law against the fruit of the SPIRIT. There will be a test on all of this stuff. It is called the rest of your life. That is your test and God is watching.

Wouldn't it be nice if Jesus came back to earth and then ran everything with the TRUTH. A world run on truth. You see God cannot lie so there is something important in always telling the truth. Truth and creation are associated. Now we return to the first page of the book. God always existed. You say; "Who made God?" I say God always existed. Try to figure out God. I just know to fear Him and obey Him. Don't fear man, fear THE ONE who can throw your soul into hell. Obey Him not just out of fear but out of love and respect.

Job 33:14-18. For God does speak—now one way, now another—though man may not perceive it. In a dream, in a vision of the night, when deep sleep falls on men as they slumber in their beds, he may speak in their ears and terrify them with warnings, to turn man from wrongdoing and keep him from pride, to preserve his soul from the pit, his life from perishing by the sword.

More things that God told me; Marriage will work if it is based on law. Cocaine leads to the grave.-That's for all of you crackheads out there! God showed me that on a tombstone—in a vision of the night. Those who go out there are submitted to the Holy Spirit. With forgiving you'll be a living sanctuary for me.—I sing this one often to myself—just as God sang it to me. Mom to go back home for some xx years. Mom almost died from all the stress and I told God that he had to tell me what was gonna happen and mom is still alive. Learning to love while you are away . . .

Acts 23:9-11. There was a great uproar, and some of the teachers of the law who were Pharisees stood up and argued vigorously. "We find nothing wrong with this man," they said. "What if a spirit or an angel has spoken to him?" The dispute became so violent that the commander was afraid Paul would be torn to pieces by them. He ordered the troops to go down and take him away from them by force and bring him into the barracks. The following night the Lord stood near Paul and said, "Take courage! As you have testified about me in Jerusalem, so you must also testify in Rome."

1 Corinthians 2:14-16. The man without the Spirit does not accept the things that come from the Spirit of God, for they are foolishness to him, and he cannot understand them, because they are spiritually discerned. The spiritual man makes judgments about all things, but he himself is not subject to any man's judgment: "For who has known the mind of the Lord that he may instruct him?" But we have the mind of Christ.

So you see, you can't just get out of jail and go nuts. When the Holy Spirit lives in you, He always helps you to do things—jobs, tasks, everyday things. At first, I would think a Spirit of God living in me? It's nothing to be afraid of. You need to invite the Holy Spirit into your life. Remember the free will? God gave us a free will to choose what to do in life. Be in line with the Spirit. Love one another as you love yourself. The human body is a great invention, so care for it—a temple of the Spirit of God. With forgiving, you'll be a living sanctuary for me. God says that you need to forgive, realize that everyone goes in front of the Son Jesus after we die. The same Spirit that rose Jesus Christ from the dead, can dwell IN you.

John 14:15-17. "If you love me, you will obey what I command. And I will ask the Father, and he will give you another Counselor to be with you forever—the Spirit of truth. The world cannot accept him, because it neither sees him nor knows him. But you know him, for he lives with you and will be in you."

John 14:26. But the Counselor, the Holy Spirit, whom the Father will send in my name, will teach you all things and will remind you of everything I have said to you.

I hope you know the Holy Spirit as I do. When I say die daily, I mean die to the flesh sinful nature. Breathe out the old self and breathe in the Spirit of God. Let not pride swell up in you as you experience the miracles and gifts of God. It is all free. Just submit to God and invite Him into your life. Finally home, and if you are preparing to go home, don't forget God. One guy went back to jail and he said that he forgot about God. Visions of the future—I would pray for. God knows everything; past, present, future. He can tell you things that you have long forgotten. Jesus said the kingdom of heaven is within you. All you can do sometimes is to plant the seed—the word of God—and hope that it multiplies.

CONCLUSION

God, I'm laughing—that's the best medicine—because I have to conclude this with the truth about the house. The bed would jump up off the ground; there are impressions in the floor. The slide bolt would move left to right a few times by itself. The cat was locked inside the cupboard when no one was in the house. A very beautiful spirit lady was seen, then she vanished.

So, I completely asked Jesus to be with me upon return from the vacation. I believe that Jesus walked in ahead of me and the demons that were here . . . He said something like-to the effect of—"Look! you all gotta go, right now . . ." His eyes lit up like fire and He had a scar bloody wound on His side where the spear got Him and a robe thing around the rest of Him . . . The party was over. They were like, "WHAT THE . . . Jesus Christ?" Bam and that was it. No more crazy poltergeists. It was all quiet. Only the rain drips in and an occasional snake. I told the one parole guy about the copper head in the living room. You people believe anything I say. But that really is true also. He don't mess with copper heads, he'd shoot it, and I'd have to clean it up. But those scary noisey ghosts were gone. I'll tell you what, Jesus could kick someones butt if He had to. I believe that He could just speak and His enemys would fall dead. All judgement has been entrusted to the Son. You better get right with Him because someday you will stand in front of Him and pay account. I remember the one older parole guy would speak of how you had to pay account and go to the meetings to show your face. I had to show my face at the bike thief hearing where I dropped the charges and had to say, "I believe mercy triumphs over judgment."

I remember my one celly saying, "Don't view my kindness as a weakness, Home!" Jails where you don't want to be. I remember you; the young juvenile delinquent reading this. I hope your mom or dad handed you this book and said, "Now don't come out of your room until you have read the whole thing! . . . And turn that radio down!"

1 Peter 1:3-9. Praise be to the God and Father of our Lord Jesus Christ! In his great mercy he has given us new birth into a living hope through the resurrection

of Jesus Christ from the dead, and into an inheritance that can never perish, spoil or fade—kept in heaven for you, who through faith are shielded by God's power until the coming of the salvation that is ready to be revealed in the last time. In this you greatly rejoice, though now for a little while you may have had to suffer grief in all kinds of trials. These have come so that your faith—of greater worth than gold, which perishes even though refined by fire—may be proved genuine and may result in praise, glory and honor when Jesus Christ is revealed. Though you have not seen him, you love him; and even though you do not see him now, you believe in him and are filled with an inexpressible and glorious joy, for you are receiving the goal of your faith, the salvation of your souls.

This is important stuff and needs to be heard by the entire world! I don't care what you think of me, it doesn't matter. If I came to spray your yard, your wife would be calling me honey and handing me money. See how you can be distracted easily? Gotta keep that focus on God and die daily to the flesh—sinful nature. It's that battle we all have of our spirit verses the flesh desires. One person likes to drink alcohol to feed their flesh, others stupidly do cocaine. That will kill you and make your heart wear out and make you rob people. The Spirit gives life.

Lamentations 3:34-36. To crush underfoot all prisoners in the land, to deny a man his rights before the Most High, to deprive a man of justice—would not the Lord see such things?

Mom will tell you about 1 in 100. Sammy will put his word in and dad wanted to but he said they would never publish it if he told them the truth of what happened.

Job 3:11. "Why did I not perish at birth, and die as I came from the womb?"

The Lord had His hand on the entire process. I believe God will repay us for all of the money lost, and then some. The one preacher said—double for the trouble.

Job 42:10. After Job had prayed for his friends, the Lord made him prosperous again and gave him twice as much as he had before.

God is LOVE and wants the best for us. Love was back in 1985. Riding in the woods, building campfires by a creek—a place we called number one. Being dense to the world and the evil of man that was lurking in the future. Life was great and it still is. The body is the greatest thing you will ever own so take care of it. Quit smoking, walk more, eat healthy foods that God made for us. Who do you think made the apple, or the orange or banana? This goes out for the ones who say there is no God. The evidence is clear—only the Lord made the bugs—some so small that you can barely see them. I wouldn't hurt a bug because it has a purpose but that time I got stung by about 20 yellow jackets, they died at night fall. I'm only human. It's not good to kill unless a big bear is chasing you through the woods to eat you! People should not be on death row. The one governor did away with it in his state because—he didn't want to put to death someone who he really didn't know—if they were guilty or not. Being in jail is bad enough.

So, why would man-kind kill you if you kill someone? That's evil for evil. Stay free is one goal of this book if you are a newly released prisoner. It gets better. A few points are worth mentioning in the light of forgiveness.

One guy—we won't say his name—but I'll give him a copy of this book, well when I was in the jail, he went to dad and says something to the effect of: That house—like when is Tony coming home ... ah?

Dad said I had like a year and a half to go—those bastards-you know they can let you out whenever they want to—so a year and a half to max out. That means to do the entire 8 years of a 4-8 year vacation. So this guy wants to buy the house where I'm sitting now typing this beautiful Jesus filled book. So dad says, "Well how much do you want to give?" The guy says he got 5 grand. Now why you gonna insult someone like that? A forth of an acre goes for $34,000 dollars. I think it is called insult on top of injury. I talked to the one property seller and they were like, "That was a real jerk move, why would he say that?" Well why does anyone say anything that they say? So it is up to you to decide to forgive.

"With forgiving, you'll be a living sanctuary for me." God the Holy Spirit-the Spirit of Christ.

It's up to you. Sometimes, I get all like—bubbly mad—we'll call it. Mad angry—not mad insane. Sam says-just don't act on it. I'll tell mom and dad, just smile and wave as we see them in their yard. Mom says she's not waving. So we talk about forgiveness. If I came home and someone was living here and sleeping here—this is a book about God, remember. You can' be all mad or resentful or giving someone a dirty look as some people do! I wave and smile. I went and talked to the people about Jesus and jail. You might be the only bible someone sees by your actions to imitate Christ. Like Sam would agree-we'll see THEM at the yard. Run to the roar, as one preacher put it.

One guy was alledgedly talking crap about me in the jail—and there is nothing worse than being treated as if you were really guilty—when you are not. So I talked to him about it—"Aint said a word about you." That's what I thought. So you see that when you are home, there is still some crap to go through. Be careful of the company that you keep or hang around. One lawyer mentioned about sleeping with dogs—you know—you might get a flea or two. You could be a woman and a man could be a dog, so I'm not saying nothing bad about women. Women are beautiful. So on a daily basis, put off the misdeeds of the flesh and put on the Holy Spirit. A forgiving heart is a big requirement. God is love and you need to have love in your heart for Him to dwell in you. Submit to God. When you do so, He helps you to figure things out. Example: You can be doing a job and if something arises that is tough to figure out, an image of the tool needed or of how to do the job—arises in my head. That is God working and His voice is always in line with scripture. So you know it is Him talking to you. That same Spirit that raised

Jesus from the dead—can dwell in you. Don't plan on using God—let God use you as a tool.

Whenever I go somewhere, I always say, "Five minutes won't go by and we will see something stupid that a person does." Always happens and I believe it is because they are not led by The Holy Spirit. Just another person trying to do it on their own—as I used to before I knew God. Either someone parks like right on the edge of the road or a person is turning around in the middle of an intersection with other cars having to stop. That's why I have full tort 'cause there are too many people who just don't think when they do things while driving. This is how the world will start to distract you from God's voice.

As far as I understand—if it is God's will for you to hear His voice, we must get the residual sin out of our lives. It's not a case of; "God aint got no rap for me!" It IS a case of: The Lord Jesus Christ opens your ear when it's in your heart to obey.

Isaiah 50:4-5. The Sovereign Lord has given me an instructed tongue, to know the word that sustains the weary. He wakens me morning by morning, wakens my ear to listen like one being taught. The Sovereign Lord has opened my ears, and I have not been rebellious; I have not drawn back.

Before we can hear from God, we must set our hearts on doing whatever He says. Obey His commands which are for our own good. Being in line with God opens new doors for personal spiritual growth. Feed your spirit with the Word of God to grow in the right direction—like a plant growing towards a light. I can't watch the news much 'cause it fills your mind with all the negative happenings. That makes you realize that THIS world is run on doctors, lawyers, judges, and they all need 'bad' things to operate. Doctor needs sickness, lawyer needs trouble, judges need trials. One old guy at the jail told me that the world is evil and needs evil to run. But praise the Lord for His Kingdom. I see a nice summer day everyday and snow if you want to ski. God—if He has a trial, His judgment is right because He is perfect and knows all of whatever happened. No one can lie in His courtroom because He really does know what did or did not happen when you hid that dead body and got yourself on death row! Only God sees all—everywhere—all the time.

Proverbs 17:15. Acquitting the guilty and condemning the innocent—the Lord detests them both.

Proverbs 15:3. The eyes of the Lord are everywhere, keeping watch on the wicked and the good.

Get right with the Lord. Ask and He will answer you. Let His reflection shine down on us and we can reflect His glory by acting and speaking like He does. People watch your behavior when you say you are a Christian. They want to see what that means, so you gotta act right and talk right. You can't have no gutter mouth swearing all the time. I heard these people putting on a roof and they just sweared every other word. I thought, "Well you can't just walk over to them and hand them a bible and be like—read this and then you won't act like that." Then people have the attitude-jail is the cure for your bad attitude or mouth, or behavior. No it's not the cure and I know all about the mission of the jail. I know all about the 8 years of Rockview, remember? "Nice and loud, so everyone in the back of the church can hear you." I remember Gene coaching me through my testimony as we practiced at the church—my podium skills. God is leading me through this book. I took a few days off and guess what God told me! God only speaks the truth. I laid down to go to sleep-the cable lock is on my 300 dollar quad, so don't get no ideas-and God said to me, "Hands for Him." That's powerful. I was probably doing some distraction that was—not typing the book-TONY! God spoke and I explained my case that the book has my personal deadline of Halloween. Here's my Halloween gift to the devil-my book. Only 'cause Jesus has my back now. The devil is a beautiful angel but God is ALL POWERFUL. God can destroy us all if He wanted to, LUCKY for us—God is love. So much to share but we need to focus on why God speaks and you don't hear Him. Your sins of the flesh are in need of disposal. Orgies and the like—the sinful nature of the flesh.

Ezekiel 12:1-2. The word of the Lord came to me: "Son of man, you are living among a rebellious people. They have eyes to see but do not see and ears to hear but do not hear, for they are a rebellious people."

John 8:42-47. Jesus said to them, "If God were your Father, you would love me, for I came from God and now am here. I have not come on my own; but he sent me. Why is my language not clear to you? Because you are unable to hear what I say. You belong to your father, the devil, and you want to carry out your fathers desire. He was a murderer from the beginning, not holding to the truth, for there is no truth in him. When he lies, he speaks his native language, for he is a liar and the father of lies. Yet because I tell the truth, you do not believe me! Can any of you prove me guilty of sin? If I am telling the truth, why don't you believe me? He who belongs to God hears what

God says. The reason you do not hear is that you do not belong to God."

Jesus explained it best. Sin separates you from God, It's your choice—your call. The blessings of the Lord are much more than the pleasures of the flesh. "Live forever, forever, forever by the Fruit.", God told me as I was nearing release. The fruit—as I interpret it—is the fruit of the Spirit.

Galatians 5:22-25. But the fruit of the Spirit is love, joy, peace, patience, kindness, goodness, faithfulness, gentleness and self-control. Against such things there is no law. Those who belong to Christ Jesus have crucified the sinful nature with its passions and desires. Since we live by the Spirit, let us keep in step with the Spirit.

A message from mom:

"I'm writing this for my son, Tony—who was in jail for 8 years for nothing. I'm now 80 years old and have congestive heart failure among other illnesses from worrying about him all those years and how mean he was treated in jail for nothing. I wrote him a letter every night for 8 years and also cried every night. He was born with Hylane membrane lung disease and 1 out of 100 babies lived. I remember when I had him, they brought everyone's baby to the mothers, but didn't bring me my son. I asked them, "Where is my baby?" They said they had to rush him to Childrens hospital before he died. He had a purpose to live. He had to write a book and tell the world how God had him make it in this world-especially in the jail. My son is a very generous and a very special person to me and he had to live for 8 years in a place no bigger than your bathroom with someone else. I hope you enjoy his book because everything he wrote is true and straight from the heart."

Thank you, his mom; Elaine.

The problem that I have is that I see mom and dad struggle daily over paying back the payoff money to the bank. Then I remember the old Italian guy. Our talk went something like this;

"Tony, TONY! the kilo's? You mentioned the kilo's? It was our secret, and a very big secret at that. But I like your book Tony. Very inspiring about our Lord and Saviour Jesus—The Christ. You know I also believe because Jesus helped me in the war. See my arm? It is plastic from here down. Blown off by a hand grenade. My ears were ringing and I fell and as I was falling down, I noticed my hand dangling. I see in your eyes Tony—you also have the trauma from life. So I came to, and a doctor was writing with his finger on my forehead—the letter M. That means they gave you morphine. My hand works perfect and I'm alive. That is only by the Lords' Grace.

Alive Tony! So enjoy life. I saw when you pulled up—I watch on my camera—and I noticed you say hi to the lovely lady. She is 25 and I pay her 2 grand a week to keep the yard nice—she likes flowers—and to . . . let's say—keep me company, if you get my drift. But the kilos Tony—I'm trusting you to say—You made that part up. OK? People in high places need to live a higher life. The Lord Jesus—He is very real and we all know that He is True.

You see I am over 60 now and we need to remember that the youngsters will be reading your book and people all over the world. We wouldn't want the young people to think that payoffs and ripoffs happen in high places—like they do. Elections are fixed—it doesn't matter who you vote for—we know the winner beforehand. The richest one.

The ballgames that I bet on—I know the winner before they win. The pro athletes—they got paid to drop the ball. Hear the roar of the crowd? That is what their lives are about.

All I ask Tony—'Hey Vinnie! bring me my wallet—it is on my dresser.' I think there is about a grand in my wallet. A grand, Tony? To help you to get things back together and to help with your book. All I ask is to be left out if—say the FEDS may have a question or two about some made up part of your book. Like you were telling me about the man who has the key for the one city lockup. The ounces of coke he would sell for 700 dollars. Everyone needs money.

'Today Vinnie, TODAY!' My son is heavy and a little slow and I am older and my patience is thinner.

You know in Amsterdam—they have live sex parties and the guys do coke mixed with Viagra, to keep up. I'll be alone with my lady—not some group—you understand Tony? Here's Vinnie now. One hundred, two, three, four . . . looks like 932 Tony. I hope your book makes you money Tony. To help your family, to fix your house—as I see you try to do that when you can. Leave the kilos for excitement and I have your word Tony.

Look on my camera—WOW. She is well worth every dollar that I pay her. She makes me feel young again. Let me know of your books progress Tony—if any souls were redirected from the fires of hell—as you say it is one of it's goals."

If this book has helped you to learn from my pain, please write and tell me. Anyone can get anyones address anyway—so it doesn't matter if I put it in my book:

Tony Morich

245 Salem Church Rd.

Belle Vernon, Pa. 15012

If you are in the jail, I'd like to hear of your story, maybe you were a victim of the system also.

Jails are needed. Society would fall apart and remember that man and woman do the best they can, in light of their financial needs.

Romans 12:1-2. Therefore, I urge you, brothers, in view of God's mercy, to offer your bodies as living sacrifices, holy and pleasing to God—this is your spiritual act of worship. Do not conform any longer to the pattern of this world, but be transformed by the renewing of your mind. Then you will be able to test and approve what God's will is—his good, pleasing and perfect will.

So don't worry who is the old Italian guy. Be concerned of who is this person named above all names—Jesus Christ. The ONLY way to God the Father. Jesus is the way, the truth and the life. Sometimes only He can help you. Jesus sent Sammy to help me. When I was a dog dropped off in the middle of no where, I learned from many that I was the 'White boy' and the 'White MAN' had me up on the mountain and didn't wanna let me out! "You's a white boy and they—the white man." The black people helped me more than the white. Aint none of us prejudice. See in the jail—there were skin heads, and they were white, and they would deal with blacks because you all in there together. Money is the medium. Kites—that is a bag of tobacco—.75 cents and you would buy, trade, sell things. Newports—gambling pack—means it has no tobacco shake inside the cellaphane. Always the teacher, Tony.

I'm showing you how the world starts to distract you from God. The money, the women—this one girl was like—"Oh my God, you're a bad boy—I gotta have you!" No. It's not a claim to fame, it's a claim to shame when you go to jail. Oh I was smart—made the Deans List at college—which is nothing. Sammy made me people smart and jail intelligent, and Jesus gives us His Holy Spirit—who takes from Jesus and gives to us. The wisdom and knowledge so you don't look like an idiot driving down the road doing stupid things.

Like the other day we went to see a friend and were in the middle of this intersection with turn signal on and this idiot runs the red light and I had to lock up the brakes! He swerves and barely missed us and he passes by us showing me his cell phone he was on saying, "I'm sorry man!" Well if you wreck into me and my 80 year old mom, you're gonna have some BIG PROBLEMS. Praise the Lord, we didn't wreck.

Few more things then we're done.

A message from Sammy;

I am Sammy Belle. I was born in Thomasville, North Carolina but was raised in Philadelphia Pa. in most of my free years. I fell with this case in July of 1980, and been here ever since. I was charged with murder and I have been fighting for my freedom ever since until this very day. I maintain innocent from day one until this very day.

Anyway, I have been in the prison system over 30 years now. I will be the first to tell you it hasn't been easy at all throughout the years. This is not a pretty place to be in (not guilty or guilty). Once you're here and the gate closes to the outside, you are on your own. The only thing you can count on is family. It goes without saying that "God" comes first in everybody's life. If not, God should come first because you're going to need him. There's no question about that.

Now when it comes to your present situation, man you are in trouble, yes real trouble straight-up. Things you must know, coming into, first in spite of what you're here for—you are in a different world. For me, my first step was the police station at 8th Race St. in Phila., then the Philadelphia Detention Center for about 3 to 4 months. Then the Big House; Homesberg Prison. Now that was the worst place I have ever been in until this day some 30 something years later.

Listen—the first thing you learn is to mind your own business because if not, it could-cost-you-your-life. My first 4 years I spent there fighting my case which I got convicted thereafter anyway. I was in 3 riots being there and I made it out alive—thank God for that. That was one rough time to deal with but I made it. Then to make matters worse, I was headed to "Homesberg's Big Brother"—Graterford, and that was another story within itself. Anyway, I stayed there the first time about 14 or 15 months. Then I went to Dallas, Pa. I spent 10 years there which was really hard for me, because I was and still am a stand-up person because I have always helped people if I could and that always seemed to get me in trouble because I speak up for other people who wouldn't speak up for themselves. I left Dallas and went to the super max lock down at Camp Hill, Pa. From there—back to Graterford, Pa and now I'm presently at Rockview, Pa. and I've been here now going on 16 years this January still fighting the case at this point. All of this is true. Continue to be strong no matter what, you heard me.

Always. Sammy Belle.

A message from Elaine—one of my two sisters;

Writing this page for my brother Tony's book has been quite difficult. When Tony went away, it was the worst experience of my life. I've tried to forget it because remembering is much too stressful. Hopefully, with time passing by, we all will feel less of the devastating effects of that fateful 8 years.

Tony is very generous, thoughtful, polite and respectful. He would give you the shirt off his back and the last dollar in his wallet. I'm very impressed with my brother for taking on the challenge of writing this book and retrospectively reliving the horrific events of 8 years in hell.

Tony's sister Elaine.

A message from Linda—my other sister;

Tony is my Baby Brother. I'm 12 years his senior. I would have to say Tony is definitely the pick of the three of us. My parents, in their 80's now, light up when Tony arrives and the sea's part when Tony enters their home. When Tony was so unjustly sent away for 8 years, I tried to be their rock. They no longer wanted to celebrate birthdays or holidays and without me pushing them to continue on, they may have laid dormant for 8 long years.

I would tell them we are going to smile and buy presents and eat holiday dinners together. I would say that Tony is away—he is not dead and will return with us. In the mean time, this is what Tony would want us to do. they reluctantly went along with my wishes, after much persuasion.

Mom's heart wanted to stop after Tony went away and she was hospitalized on and off for nearly a year. Tony never knew of her condition at the time. We told him after her semi-recovery. I tried to write Tony positive and uplifting words in my letters.

Not only did my parents health deteriorate, so did his house. The roof leaked, causing water damage to all his belongings. The weeds and grass grew out of control. Windows were broken out by robbers and a lot of his valued treasures were thrown out into the yard. His truck became a home to mice and rusted into the mud.

I see Tony everyday since his return home. I am always greeted with a big smile and a heartfelt, "How ya' doin', Lin'?" I reply, "Ah, I'm O.K." and he tells me how I need Jesus in my life. My reply is, "Ah, Jesus Tony!" He says, "Jesus—that's the guy that saved me!". I sigh. Now that is a common phrase between us. Tony's belief-and Sammy—got him through the 8 years of being innocent in a horrible place. My wonder is why Jesus would let this happen to our family.

On the tenth anniversary of 9-11, everyone asks what were you doing? I was on my way to visit Tony at the prison. I heard of the devastation while in a restaurant having breakfast. We returned to our car for the next hour drive and listened to the radio about what was happening to our country. All the inmates—who believed in God—prayed for our country and the lives lost. It was a very sad day, having to leave Tony behind.

Every visit to the prison was hard. Tony wore a brown jumpsuit with DOC on his back. He would sit in the visit area and smile and talk about what he was going to do upon his return. He would always say how he was going to take care of mom and dad. I thought to myself—when he see's what had become of his house, his priorities would be to fix that mess but he has put mom and dad first always. Always arriving at their house with food and a candy bar for everyone. Very generous, though he has very little. Willing to give you his last penny or the shirt off of his back if needed. Says he's happy to be outside no matter how cold or hot the weather might be.

The night the verdict came in and Tony was so unjustly sent away is a feeling I'll never forget. The same feeling comes over me right now as I recall these memories. It was bitterly cold. As we walked out of the courthouse to the car, ice was falling from the sky and stinging my face as it hit me. The snow crunched under our shoes as we tried to get in the car that was frozen shut. Tony has mostly overcome this tragedy somehow with a warm smile to everyone and a large helpful heart to all, but I still feel the ice hitting my face while writing this.

Linda.

We need to rap it up. A few more issues I need to mention: While in jail you wait for appeals and receive therapy. These go hand in hand. My appeal was lost and misfiled at the wrong court—all the while as my mom would call the one lawyer and he would—every week—tell her all was well and going as scheduled. I had the other lawyer watching him and the truth came out. My appeal was lost for about 6 years. This is why lawyers get killed, and I preach forgiveness. I was forced to stay in jail the entire 8 years. This brings further judgment on them from Jesus Christ, and more need on my end to forgive.

Next? Therapy. People who we won't name . . . They basically said—Can't fix what aint broke. "You had the perfect childhood . . . this is all very strange . . . the appeal should overturn your case." The one person actually told me; "Now that you see it works like this, don't do it to no one when you get out." Meaning—don't lie and put someone in jail.

All very shocking—to the point that it gave my mom congestive heart failure from the shock of being lied to every week. All very true. So these are things that I never knew went on, until I became a victim of the system. I think they don't view you as human beings, as from the so what, who cares—that I heard a lot of spoken on crucifixation day.

So I'm making a fire in my wood burner and I see that the one judge has had another death threat. It was in the burn paper from mom and dad. So I talk to dad and he says, "Well what does that character expect? Cases go in front of him that should not even be in front of him and they just find you guilty with no evidence."

I take it very serious—The destruction of Tony. They killed the person that I was and only Jesus Christ saved their lives. This is why I preach forgiveness. I was there wanting to kill and go on a murderous rampage because some people believe it is the only thing that you can do to them. They are immune from being sued. They can do whatever they want. You can appeal their decision. We did. Cases do get over turned. Mine would have been if the good lawyer was still on the case. The money ran out, then you're burnt.

It's tough to preach Christ when the evil of man still lingers on in the form of a bank payment from a payoff gone bad. You can't do anything to them. This is why court houses have metal detectors and armed guards. Do we need to wonder why? Some people that I talked to figure—you can't hide at the court house forever! You get in a car and drive home—look over your shoulder as you pull into your drive, lock the garage door and set the security cameras and live in complete fear from all of the people that you sent to jail! Not knowing if they were really guilty or not. The one DA was never found. Why would you make people want to kill you? Then when a judge gets gunned down—they have on tv, people saying, He was a fair man, bla bla bla. My one person I met told me, "I can't say nothing about them—they kept my boy out of a lot of trouble." Sure! 'Cause the payoff went through in his situation!

Where were we? God. God is the only ONE who can help you. He is a very present help in a time of need. Remember the things we spoke of: God the Father, God the Son Jesus, and God the Holy Spirit.

One of my comforts is knowing that these pieces of crap—Hey! that's not Christ-like Tony! Ok let me rephrase it. These big pieces of crap will go in front of Jesus Christ someday and be judged for what they did to me. My conscious is clear. My one friend told me, "Hey Tony, it's better that you write a book instead of all of you at the cementary on the same day! Then God would throw you into hell." He is RIGHT. I wouldn't even hurt a bug.

So we see the evil of man. The Glory of the LORD shines on. We see TONY don't wanna go to hell. That's what they count on. Do whatever they want to you and hope that you fear hell and spare them their lives. I lived in a cell with real life killers and murderers. There's a difference. This is all part of the healing process. Keep the focus on the Lord.

Dad says the problem is that they put you in front of a jury and they don't know you and they are not allowed to hear all of the story. At least that is what happened to me. Remember Paul in the bible?

Paul was a man—who was first called Saul—and he would persecute the Christians. He had legal papers from the law makers way back then—to take Christians to jail and or to kill them. Same as today—they have papers then they think they are doing the right thing—same as back then. So Paul was walking along with his soldiers and basically got knocked on his ass by JESUS CHRIST! Jesus saw his zeal for doing evil and told Paul what he must do. Paul was blind for three days from the light of the Lord. Jesus sent a man to lay hands on Paul and restore his sight. Paul became a great preacher of Jesus Christ.

Acts 9:1-20. Meanwhile, Saul was still breathing out murderous threats against the Lord's disciples. He went to the high priest and asked him for letters to the synagogues in Damascus, so that if he found any there who belonged to the Way, whether men or women, he might take them as prisoners to Jerusalem. As he neared Damascus on his journey, suddenly a light from heaven flashed around him. He fell to the ground and heard a voice say to him, "Saul, Saul, why do you persecute me?"

"Who are you, Lord?" Saul asked.

"I am Jesus, whom you are persecuting," he replied. "Now get up and go into the city, and you will be told what you must do."

The men traveling with Saul stood there speechless; they heard the sound but did not see anyone. Saul got up from the ground, but when he opened his eyes he could see nothing. So they led him by the hand into Damascus. For three days he was blind, and did not eat or drink anything. In Damascus there was a disciple named Ananias. The Lord called to him in a vision, "Ananias!"

"Yes, Lord," he answered.

The Lord told him, "Go to the house of Judas on Straight Street and ask for a man from Tarsus named Saul, for he is praying. In a vision he has seen a man named Ananias come and place his hands on him to restore his sight."

"Lord," Ananias answered, "I have heard many reports about this man and all the harm he has done to your saints in Jerusalem. And he has come here with authority from the chief priests to arrest all who call on your name."

But the Lord said to Ananias, "Go! This man is my chosen instrument to carry my name before the

Gentiles and their kings and before the people of Israel. I will show him how much he must suffer for my name."

Then Ananias went to the house and entered it. Placing his hands on Saul, he said, "Brother Saul, the Lord—Jesus, who appeared to you on the road as you were coming here—has sent me so that you may see again and be filled with the Holy Spirit." Immediately, something like scales fell from Saul's eyes, and he could see again. He got up and was baptized, and after taking some food, he regained his strength. Saul spent several days with the disciples in Damascus. At once he began to preach in the synagogues that Jesus is the Son of God.

Afro told me—"It's not the fall that matters anymore—because we all fall down. It's what you do AFTER the fall, that matters." Saul fell—then he followed Jesus. Jesus told me himself, "With forgiving, you'll be a living sanctuary, for me." So you see that I struggle with forgiving them all for the evil done to me. But you say—"Tony! look how good that you turned out from all of the jail! You are now a messenger from the Lord! You should thank the judge!" Uh-huh.

Less of me and more of you Lord Jesus Christ. Amen.

This is for the CRIME PREVENTION—aimed at the young juvenile delinquent who may be eye-ing up my 300 dollar quad with the cable lock on it at night. There is only one thing that bothers me to this very day. Alongside of course—of the 1000 dollar a month bank payment from the payoff that went bad. The one thing—the girlfriend that I had left me. Now we can cry about that along with all of the other guys who had their sad story about their woman. I heard every story in jail. Scott told me, "Tony, it's been 21 years and I'm still not over the woman that left me."

I think that closure is needed, as preacher man—as I call him—will step up and put a few words in to close the book for us.

So I was down at Western Pennitentary and we were locked down for 3 days as we arrived there. This single cell was so small that you could not stretch out your arms to your sides. The toilet was like a foot wide and a miniature sink that trickled out water was there with you. Cement walls and iron bars were your new friends. They—the ones in charge—would open your doors, all at once and would have set your food tray down on the floor and you would step out and look left to right at the other suffering prisoners, and pick up your food and sit on your bed and eat 3 times a day. The doctors would walk around and ask if "you OK in there?" The guy in the cell next to me couldn't take it and they took him to the hospital. Very difficult for the big heavier prisoners, is an understatement.

So on one of the nights, my beautiful girlfriend was with me in her spirit/soul body. I was half awake and as I opened my eyes, I saw her there all dazzling and sparkling next to me. That was the most beautiful thing that I have and probably will ever see. So she waited for 8 months of jail. Then she said that she couldn't do it no more. I couldn't blame her, she had to live her life. Now she is married to someone else in another state—or so I am told. I know there are more women—millions—as the old Italian guy tells me. But when there is a special kind of love—I don't know if you ever get over it.

That nice woman that you have right now—how long will she wait if you go to jail? "I'll never leave you.", "It's you and me forever." Some women wait. If I had a million dollars—she would have waited! This is reason enough right here for crime prevention. You don't want to lose that woman you got. I didn't want to lose mine. I even called her house when I got home—it was all just like I was here yesterday. Her mom answers the phone and says that she was not around here no more and hung up the phone on me. All my lady would say was that she just needed me home and well I'M HOME! Where ya' at? Obviously things ended in her mind long ago as she left the jail that day. So you need closure on different topics. Everyday—the jail memory trauma goes through my mind. Flashbacks and panic/ anxiety that the Lord is healing me of. Remember—The Lord is mighty to save. This book is healthy for me to help me to move on. I need to remember where I came from but also for it to make me stronger and a better person from it, and to never go back. Been there, did it. Tony—the old self died there. My friends there would call me Tony Diamond. Letting the light of Jesus shine through me in such a dark place. A diamond is formed under great pressure and heat. Without Jesus, I'm like a piece of dried up brush ready to be thrown into the fire. But with God, ALL things are possible. I can do all things through Christ who strengthens me. I can let the jail go—but I'll still write to my friends. I can let Nicole go. Before God gives you what he has for you, you have to let go of what you are holding on to. Closure is needed and time-with Jesus—helps you to heal. The Lord is always mighty to save. Turn to Him and he will heal you.

Psalm 94:19. When anxiety was great within me, your consolation brought joy to my soul.

THE LAST CHAPTER

It is November 16, 2011. Lets go back to October 23, 2011. I was helping my friend and the call came. My niece Annie calls and said, "Mum mum passed out and the ambulance took her to the hospital." I asked her to keep me posted. Knowing that mom can't go yet. She had lots of time!

Ten minutes later, dad calls and I knew it wasn't good. He says, "Tone, she passed away." I never heard so much pain in a mans voice before. I told him I'd be right there. So I'm driving and I'm praying and I'm crying. "Please Lord Jesus, PLEASE! You can do ALL things—you brought Lazarus back from the dead! PLEASE! I'm crying and praying and dad calls and says. "They have a weak pulse." We got this Lord—we got this. YOU GOT THIS.

So I get to the emergency room and I'm all hopeful. Everyone else arrived and after an hour or less, the Dr. lady took us into a room. No! So she looks at

ME and told all of us that they did all they could for mom. She said it just never happens that the person comes back to life and mom started breathing on her own. The Lord let her come back but the heart was wore out and beat it's last beat. Jesus showed us and me that He heard my prayer as I was driving. Linda says, "I have to see my mom—WHERE IS SHE?"

We all sat and waited in the waiting room, then after a bit, the lady said to go to room #4. I was first to the spot, and it just didn't feel like mom was there. I turned and looked at Linda and she tells the others, "She's in here."

I went over and kneeled by the right side of the bed and held mom's hand and cried for 1 hour straight. Dad stood there and had his hands on mom's feet and Linda cried and Elaine was in shock, and Annie cried.

Eighty years of love just went to heaven. I was telling mom that the book is coming and I'm gonna help you and dad and we'll make it, mom. I never knew so much pain could exist. It was worse then a thousand years in jail. I had a dream of hearing my soul screaming out in agony over mom. I still cry everyday, I guess that I need to. We all help each other through it now.

The funeral home. Lots of people showed their respect. The cementary—words you don't want to use.

Dad wanted to go back to the cemetary the next day after the burial. "Moms not at the cemetary, dad, but I'll take you." He wanted to get a few of the flowers. So it is raining and dad wanted me to straighten the dirt—mud—along the side of the grave. So I'm fixing the mud with my boot and dad says he is going to the truck. I hear this horrible scream and dad fell and hit his back and head, and I run over to him and put my arm under his back. He didn't want a Dr. or a hospital. Help us Jesus!

All the neighbors brought food and stuff, and our church lady Nancy spoke for mom at the funeral service. We need to send a lot of thank you's. I know mom made it to a better world. A few nights after mom passed, I was awakened by someone grabbing my left foot, and I heard a voice—"It's me." It was mom. The light inside of Elaine's car started to go on and off by itself. One night, Linda was over at moms and she looks at me and says, "Well isn't mom gonna turn on the light for ME? I'm here now."

On that day that mom went, she was in her kitchen painting her fingernails getting ready for the flea market. Her left hand was done and she fell to the floor, and Annie tried to catch her. Dad was down in the garage. Mom lived her life to the very last second, taking care of herself. I saw the monitor screen with that flat line at the E.R.—it said unit disconnected.

Until it is YOUR mom laying there—you'll never understand the pain. I would never even want to think of the day without mom.

About a week ago, we were all over on dad's porch and I told dad, Linda and Elaine that I think I've suffered some type of damage from all of this. My heart is doing this weird dancing around. Dad says, "That's just your nervous system!" Dad says, "LISTEN—all three of you—you and you and you (he looked at each of us)—STRAIGHTEN UP! Mom don't want to see all of you like this. For thousands of years, people have gotten married, had families and the older ones die. Then the younger ones grow up and THEY die. This has been going on now for thousands of years. This is how life is."

Mom told us when we were little kids that people in Finland-she was 100% Finlander—they celebrate when someone dies because they made it to a better world. God willing. The day after mom passed, she went to dad first as he was sleeping on the chair in the living room. He was happy to tell us, "Mom came to me and she was real young and pretty and smiling—like she was 35 again." Thats what mom told us heaven would be like—everyone is 35 again.

Back in 2006, God told me, "Mom to go back home for some 12 years." So I thought it was 2006 plus 12 is 2018. Now I believe my perception was cloudy and it was ". . . some twelveth year. I didn't hear the th on twelve. Some twelfth year was October 23, 2011. I'm a human under the curse of Adam and we all make errors. I claim the blood of Jesus. I was in so much pain for the first week that I was calling out to God to ease my pain for me and the family. Angels ministered to me. I heard the most beautiful music ever as I was waking up for the day. The Lord giveth, the Lord taketh away, blessed be the name of the Lord. I said that as I was holding moms hand. Death has no grip on me for I have eternal life with the Lord. Mom has made it to heaven and we will see her again. I'm ready to go now if the Lord wants me. Right after mom went—I told God that he can take me. I know I'll be judged for it but I told God on that first night, "You wanna take somebody—TAKE ME!" I would gladly have went. Strike me down-put me in the ground, it just doesn't even matter anymore. When you have that attitude—God won't take ya'. I didn't curse God, I just didn't want mom to go.

You are a spirit in a flesh body, that's what keeps you in the world. We are subjected to the elements. Rain, wind, sun light, cold and hot, these are things in this world. This is SOUL DIRECTION. If you are bad, you either go to jail or hell. God don't wanna send no one to hell-it was made for the devil—But if you go nuts and start killin'—you might go to hell.

Death of a family member is up there with the stress of a jail sentence.

The Angel of death was all around our area where we live, as I will explain.

The Angel of death was all around this area. The guy across the road passed away first, then a neighbor lady next door, then I felt this presence come upon me as I was in the shower. I could not breathe! No air in or out. Couldn't talk but I prayed "God, please don't let me die in the shower! Naked." This terrible death presence was all around, taking the weaker ones. I know it is true, then a cop was running at the one neighbor—aiming a gun at him. Death was all around.

Mom has shed her skin and moved on to the next world. I know she made it to heaven. Her of all people had the best chance. Bob told me that I did a great job at bringing mom to church and getting her closer to knowing God. The last paragraph begins again today on December 15, 2011. That is today. It seems Christmas now begins December 1. Praise The Lord. I'm fighting this book again for obvious reasons. I've had this terrible head ache for 4 days now so I'm hoping if I type The Lords book here, that God will subside my pain. These people on the news that say about God tells them to go kill . . . I disagree. God will speak in line with His Word—the bible. God is Love. Love one another. What the hell is wrong with the world! Live forever by the Fruit—The Fruit of the Spirit. I know I'm the devils enemy—I told him to his face that I'm done with him, in the spirit world of course. So we are trapped in this body until we die. The bible tells us that no murderer has eternal life in him. So, you can't kill NOBODY, not even yourself! I know mom is in heaven. God has showed all of my family this. Mom came to dad first. She grabbed my foot as I was sleeping. Elaines car light was going on and off. Dad and I were going to a store and he was going on about mom this and mom that and we heard a loud—glass smashing noise—in the back seat as we were driving along. I looked back and said, "What the HELL was THAT!?" Dad says, "Mum." It was like a glass window exploded for 4 seconds. The car has a rag top. Praise the Lord and if I wanna see mom—I can't kill no damn body! I gotta live until I die. We all gonna die! "Don't be scared now—you weren't scared when you were on the blue goose!"—I would hear the one prisoner at the jail say this a lot. To tell the truth—Mom going to heaven almost KILLED ME! If I think about it I get a terrible pain in my heart! LORD HELP US!

I talked to Sam—the guy on the cover. I cried the whole way through it. He said, "I'm the one with the broad shoulders." Sam wants me to realize that The Lord took mom home. In his card he wants me to man up. Linda and I talked and she says that she needs to WOMAN up. I never knew that so much pain existed. You was once in your moms body as a baby. The Lord knit you together in moms womb. That's why it is so painful when mom went and because mom was and is the greatest mom. It is so difficult when such a great love exists and is separated by 2 worlds. That's reason enough for me not to kill the judge! I say this for all of you future killers out there. I would rather be with mom than burn in hell, and you should feel the same. OK Lord I'm typing—please take this head ache away! They told me it is my book—my way, so "fall back from the gate ole-head and relax." So they say in the jail. Remember the one guy told me, "Whatever they doin' here—they sure doin' it right because—I HATE THIS PLACE!" Mark would tell me, "Why ME, Tone? Why do I have to have the ten to twenty?" This is CRIME PREVENTION and SOUL DIRECTION. Remember the test is coming up, it's called the rest of your life. God says to forgive, so He can forgive you. Love one another and don't kill nobody—don't hurt nobody. Live by the FRUIT OF THE SPIRIT. Hands for Him, and help someone like Sam helped me. Afro helped me too. The White people sent me to the jail, and the black people helped me through it.

I was in a dorm on the honor block and I was the only white guy in an all black dorm. I was the one white out of 17 blacks. We all respected each other. Respect is something you learn in prison or you get the lock in the sock. If you have a problem with your mouth—that can be fixed. It's called the lock in the sock treatment. I lifted weights for 8 years and read a LOT of bible. Jesus is the only Way that I made it. Remember your reason to make it to heaven—to be with your loved ones who have gone on before you. Help some body. Love one another. Forgive, which is a topic I struggle with. 8 years for a crime that I did not commit. You have to move on with Jesus as your Rock. Base your relationships on The Lord and they will last. Crucify the flesh on a daily basis and the desires thereof. Live for The SPIRIT. Daily praying for an indwelling of the Holy Spirit is required. Overcome evil with good—snuff it out at the beginning. Put God first as I am now, and the Lord will bless you. This is the life that you have so make the best of it, no matter where or when you are.

I've told you about JESUS CHRIST—the final JUDGE. The Blessed HOLY SPIRIT, and GOD THE FATHER. We know of our enemy—the devil.

Vengance belongs to the Lord. May the Lord protect you from any evil.

It is finished.

THE ANGEL I heard an angel call me and take me by the hand.

So when tomorrow starts without me, you will understand.

The Angel said my place was ready in heaven far above, and I would have to leave behind all those I dearly loved.

The Fall, the Spring and Summer and all the winters' ice; I won't miss it at all, because in Heaven, it will be so nice.

So if you believe in Angels and one takes you by the hand, we will all be together in this beautiful promise land.

So when I'm gone, please think of me and know we'll never part, because an angel took me by the hand, but I'll be in your heart.

Written by mom, March 8, 2006.

IN CLOSING

My book, my way-more to say—now a very brief extra closing to the book. A police officer was just killed during a routine traffic stop. Today is Christmas December 25, 2011. Happy birthday Jesus. Remember that this book is CRIME PREVENTION, SOUL DIRECTION and also to help save the lives of police officers, judges, and people all over the world. Judges run their mouths and co-sign for things because they think they can do whatever they want. The world needs to know that this book is a very true life story. All of it is true but I am forced to list it as a work of fiction ONLY for legal reasons. I don't wanna hear nobody cryin' about—"Tony told on us!" I heard enough damn cryin' from all of my cellys for EIGHT DAMN YEARS! You took the 50 grand and didn't do what you were supossed to do. Now you have a problem with the Lord—not me. I suffer watching dad—now alone with us—struggle to pay back the payoff money. He has 30 months to go at 1000 dollars a month. He just wants to live 30 months to see how it is to not be in debt. Mom died a poor person, but rich in faith. It is only Jesus Christ as the reason I am not in hell now. This is why I preach against killing, and why the police officer who just got killed is forcing me to write and type more.

Officer down! He got shot 'cause he was gonna have a guy's vehicle towed. I wasn't there—I don't know what happened, as only God knows the terrible details. He got shot again in the head—probably to stop the screams. Don't let no ones mouth-push you to kill or act like a nut. Jesus says that if we hold anger towards a person that we are in danger of the hell fire. The shooter drove home and the SWAT team was soon at his house. Now you have the choice to surrender or die. I know the guy who lived next door—now he has trauma for life also. 300 rounds of gun fire? Tear gas shot through the window, a percussion flash grenade, the guy was killed. I don't believe murder is the answer—there has to be a better way rather than evil for evil. Everyone I talk to has an opinion about it. Better behave or we'll send our black truck with guns after you! We have the right to be safe in society, this is why I stress the importance of praying daily for an indwelling of The Holy Spirit. Jesus said to LOVE ONE ANOTHER. The command is simple. Do not be overcome by evil—overcome evil with good. My one friend said to me, "If I'm gonna open up a can of whoop ass, don't start throwing Holy Water on me!"

You never know what anyone is going through at certain times so don't piss 'em off! Some people have lost it all and don't be the straw that broke the camels back. No one needs to hear MAN DOWN. If someone killed YOU, the cops would go after them with the black death truck. They are all allowed to murder you and it is ok—if you were the killer.

Remember to guard your heart and especially your soul. You have been bought with a price—the blood of Jesus Christ. You belong to Him. God knitted you together in your mothers womb and your soul is from God. We are only passing through this world on earth and I'm thankful for that. You are born and you will die, then the Judgment. God will ask as He knows the answer—something like—what have you done with the life I have given you? Did you hurt or did you help? Did you tell someone about Jesus? I did. He is the ONLY way, truth, life. Stay in the Word of God and you will have peace.

Look how tragic mom going to heaven was. Heavens eternal gain and our loss—has occured to our family. Jesus said that the kingdom of heaven is within you. The soul goes back to God who gave it. The soul is only put in the physical body until your body dies. You are trapped in your body—same as I am. Enjoy it! Live life to the very last beat of your heart—as my mom did. She had the fingernails on one hand painted red, then her heart stopped. Our world was crushed but we are not defeated because our hope is in The Lord Jesus Christ. Mom is with Jesus in HEAVEN! Praise the Lord. I wanna go to heaven more than I want to take out a piece of crap judge who doesn't know how to talk to people the right way. That's why this book is listed as a fiction—all they know is evil for evil in this evil world. That is why JESUS CHRIST is the only hope that we have in this life.

John 16:33 "I have told you these things, so that in me you may have peace. In this world you will have trouble. But take heart! I have overcome the world."